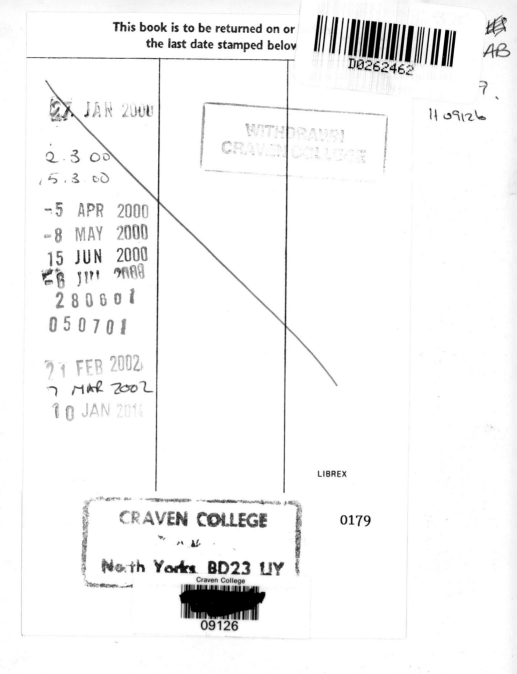

This book is to be returned on or
the last date stamped below

COMPETENCE AND ACCOUNTABILITY IN EDUCATION

This is the first volume of a series to be entitled

Monitoring Change in Education

Competence and Accountability in Education

edited by

Peter McKenzie

Philip Mitchell

Paul Oliver

arena

Published by
Arena
Ashgate Publishing Limited
Gower House
Croft Road
Aldershot
Hants GU11 3HR
England

Ashgate Publishing Company
Old Post Road
Brookfield
Vermont 05036
USA

British Library Cataloguing in Publication Data

Competence and Accountability in Education
   I. McKenzie, Peter
   370
ISBN 1 85742 279 1

Library of Congress Catalog Card Number: 95-76328

Printed and bound in Great Britain by
Hartnolls Limited, Bodmin, Cornwall

Contents

Notes on contributors

(Contributors are based at the School of Education of the University of Huddersfield, except where otherwise indicated.)

David Brady has taught science in the UK and in Nigeria. This has given him an interest in all aspects of the curriculum, particularly as they relate to technical and vocational education.

Bob Butroyd is a senior lecturer in Business Education in Initial Teacher Education. His research interests cover recent developments in teacher education with particular reference to competency-based training.

Mary Jane Drummond is a tutor in primary education at the University of Cambridge Institute of Education. She writes as an experienced infant teacher, headteacher and in-service educator.

Christine Johnson is a senior lecturer in Curriculum and Academic Management in a large college of further education in the North-East. She has been concerned with establishing and maintaining quality in further education, particularly in the areas of NVQ and GNVQ provision.

Peter McBride is a principal lecturer in Education and author of a book and many articles on educational policy, training and local government.

Peter McKenzie has taught in further and adult education and in recent years has lectured in the Philosophy of Education to teachers in training.

Philip Mitchell taught modern languages and worked in educational administration before moving to his present post in teacher education. Currently he has a particular interest in political and organisational issues as they relate to education.

David Neve is a construction group tutor with an interest in competence and its assessment.

Paul Oliver has published articles on multicultural education and most recently he has written on the subject of credit accumulation and transfer systems in higher education.

Lewis Owen works in teacher education. He has a background in school-teaching and further, higher and adult education. His research interests centre around language and learning, and social theory and institutional change.

John Sheehan has been involved in Nurse Education and Nurse Teacher Education for many years, and has published numerous papers on these issues.

Foreword

Technical teacher-training was proposed by the McNair Report: Teachers and Youth Leaders (1944), and in 1947 one of three national centres for the training of technical teachers was established in Huddersfield under the direction of Alexander MacLennan.

Generations of teachers will know Holly Bank as the site in Huddersfield where technical teacher-training began, and this now continues as the campus for the University's School of Education. Over the years enrolment has grown to more than 2,000 British and overseas teachers on Huddersfield programmes, which range from the Certificate in Education to PhD studies. These developments have generated a large body of expertise, and I was therefore extremely pleased when my colleagues proposed to publish a series of papers intended to complement the enlarged environment of teaching and research now characterising the activities of the School.

Since 1947 there have been many innovations, some more enduring than others, but I have no doubt that one of the most profound issues at the present time is that of competency-based training, which stresses the importance of training for the workplace. The emphasis is now very much on equipping people for the 'real world' and on the cost-effective achievement of standards of performance, implying some overshadowing of considerations of knowledge and theory, and this, of course, has consequences for how teachers are viewed as being accountable.

Recent research studies have questioned the efficacy of the new approach, and now my colleagues and others are collectively attempting in the papers which follow to illuminate the different perspectives as a contribution to the debate. Most teachers who attend Holly Bank have views on the current scene, and tutors are in a privileged position to be able to debate the issues with them. There can be no doubt that competency-based training has been the subject of much searching discussion of late, and these papers, expressing views honed by experience, are very appropriate at this time. For the future we plan that contributions of equal significance and relevance will be published, and it is with great pleasure and confidence that I present this collection to you.

Eric Twigg
Dean of the School of Education, The University of Huddersfield

Preface

'Competence' and 'accountability' are concepts of great current significance in education. 'Competence', an idea with a complex and interesting history, has had prominence and perhaps notoriety thrust upon it in the last few years as a result of its adoption as a 'term of art' by the National Council of Vocational Qualifications (NCVQ). This liaison has given rise to the eponymous, if unofficial, 'Competence movement', while the term 'competence' itself has become a code-word that calls into question much of what education has traditionally seen itself as achieving, and the way in which it achieves it. Notably, in the context of vocational education, the Competence movement focuses on the 'can-do' aspects of learning, arguably to the detriment of knowledge, understanding, and all-round development. Intense debates rage round the ideological and pedagogical issues implicit in this change of emphasis; what is certain is that this is no trivial matter but, rather, one that has implications reaching far beyond the questions of teaching method that might seem to be at issue.

To an extent, this wider significance is made evident by the way in which schools and the trainers of teachers increasingly experience pressure to conceptualise learning in ways that would be congenial to the Competence movement. The National Curriculum in effect endorses outcomes, a notion dear to the heart of NCVQ; while teacher education moves steadily towards a regime of training located in schools, that is, in the workplace; where, it is assumed, true 'competence' is to be found. It could be argued that we are in the middle of a cultural revolution. Is it good or bad? creative iconoclasm or wanton barbarism? or a mixture of these things? These papers address that question.

'Accountability', meanwhile, is something that teachers and lecturers have tended to regard as a function of their professionalism. It has not, hitherto, meant detailed compliance with a set of instructions but, rather, the interpretation of a code. The Competence movement seems much more interested in a bureaucratic model of accountability and, arguably, the notion of competence and its operationalisation serve to promote this latter model over the former. 'Accountability' is coming to have overtones on the whole very different from those it has held for teachers in the past: the pursuit of a certain concept of competence greatly facilitates this shift of meaning.

The papers in this book explore these topics at different levels of detail and analysis. DAVID BRADY's chapter provides a wide-ranging survey of competence-based education. He notes the problematic areas that have been identified, particularly the emphasis on outcomes at the expense of knowledge and educational experience. In unintentionally ironic comment upon this emphasis, and with close reference to particular cases, CHRISTINE JOHNSON and DAVID NEVE consider, respectively, the wide discrepancies produced by different assessors when given the same evidence to assess in a (purportedly objective) NVQ exercise; and the anomalies, and costs, involved in accrediting experienced lecturers as assessors through TDLB standards. JOHN SHEEHAN deals with the issue of competence, and associated difficulties, in a nursing context at the Pre-Registration, Post-Registration and Health Care Assistant levels; and, attempting some degree of arbitration between different views. PETER McKENZIE and PAUL OLIVER discuss the recent Smithers Report - a powerful critique of the Competence movement - and the NCVQ response to this; concluding that the issues surrounding knowledge content and quality remain unresolved, and are indeed further blurred by the naturalistic framework of NVQ design.

Relating such issues to that of accountability, BOB BUTROYD explores models of teacher education, interpretations of competence, and the application of social market principles to education. He offers a view of teacher education which encourages teachers' professional judgement and promotes teacher autonomy. PHILIP MITCHELL likewise examines the implications of the growth of accountability for the professional life of teachers, arguing that recent and current developments risk undermining, rather than enhancing, the effectiveness of teachers; and, vividly illustrating his thesis, MARY JANE DRUMMOND holds the concept of competence up against what she knows of primary education, and examines what she sees as its inadequacies, omissions and distortions.

PETER McBRIDE reviews the legislation that has made recent 'reforms' possible, and argues that the 1993 Education Act will not resolve long-standing debates, but will resurrect old divisions and create anomalies that will render it, unlike its 1902 and 1944 predecessors, inadequate to provide a settlement for a generation, let alone an epoch.

Finally, LEWIS OWEN presents an alternative and perhaps corrective perspective. He argues that, while criticisms of National Vocational Qualifications are largely justified, strong support for some of the new developments, in the light of the requirements of the global economy and of the need to change traditional patterns of power in education, is essential. If we do not make the system work we must resign ourselves to a rapid slide into semi-industrialisation and a 'brazilianisation' of the economy.

The above papers, then, raise questions of fundamental importance concerning what has become little less than a revolution, both in the field of vocational training and in that of general education. The outcomes of this revolution, progressive or reactionary as they may be, will determine the nature of our educational culture and, increasingly, will influence our standards of living and our global role in years to come and perhaps for ever. We would do well to ponder the questions carefully, answer them judiciously, and act, where we can, with a full sense of the responsibility that all involved in the project of educating and training must carry.

This editorial preface would not be complete without a mention, with our best thanks, of the considerable - indeed indispensable - help we have received from a number of colleagues in the University, including those providing administrative and secretarial support. We wish to express our gratitude for the guidance readily available to us from colleagues on the Editorial Board of the University's School of Education. In this connection we are particularly grateful to Dr Yves Benett, Chair of the Board, and to Professor Cedric Cullingford. Without the backcloth of their expertise and enthusiasm this whole venture would have been much the poorer.

1 Competence-based education

David Brady

Abstract

The paper discusses the rapid growth of competence-based approaches to curriculum planning, in particular in regard to recent developments such as NVQs and GNVQs. It notes the concerns which have been expressed about these approaches. 'Competence' is an elusive concept. What at first sight appears to be a useful and commonsense idea is found, on further reflection, to be complex and possibly misleading. In particular, the relationship between competence and knowledge is controversial.

The use of competence statements is related to earlier attempts (notably through the use of behavioural objectives) to give clear expression to curriculum intentions. It is suggested that an emphasis on competence expressed as outcomes results in a narrow view of education and even of employment.

The concluding part of the paper notes that experience is an important part of education. It is wrong to assume that some students, because of their actual or intended occupations, need only practical 'competencies'.

Introduction

Having originated in teacher education in the United States, competence-based approaches to education and training have crossed the Atlantic and, in a relatively short period of time, have become a dominant influence in vocational education in the United Kingdom.

> Competency-based education has been shown to be most effective as an alternative to conventional forms of education. (Finch and Crunkilton, 1989, p241)

1

Rather more dramatically, Fennell (1990, p2) likens the introduction of competence-based standards to events which had recently occurred in Eastern Europe! 'Once the floodgates of reform are opened, the power of new ideas can force the pace of change with dramatic speed'. However, not everyone is convinced that it is the power of the idea which is leading to the rapid change.

Despite some misgivings in academic circles, competence-based education is spreading into higher education and this rapid dissemination indicates a highly significant development but one which raises a number of important questions. These include:

1   What are the practical benefits and drawbacks of a competence-based approach to assessment and to curriculum development?
2   Does the approach carry any 'ideological baggage' in that it reflects a particular view concerning the purpose of education; and does it tend to exclude alternative views?
3   Does the rapid spread of the competence-based approach into various sectors of education indicate a broad consensus in its favour, or is it to be seen as a managerial imposition on unwilling teachers?

This paper will concentrate mainly on the first two of these major questions. In turn these questions will lead to consideration of further issues such as the historical background and antecedents of this approach to curriculum development.

The rapid spread of competence-based approaches should not be taken as an indication that they command universal or even widespread support. As will be seen, they have been criticised on a number of grounds including behaviourism, reductionism and atomisation. Hardly surprisingly, the publications of official bodies such as the National Council for Vocational Qualifications (NCVQ) tend to be generally enthusiastic. 'Under the surface', despite the large numbers of teachers working hard to develop and implement competence-based approaches, there is considerable confusion and disagreement. This came to public attention when the Smithers Report (1993) on Channel 4 Television raised some serious concerns about the competence-based National Vocational Qualifications (NVQs) and provoked a sharp response from the NCVQ (1993). It may well be argued that a television documentary is not the best or the correct way in which to conduct an educational debate but it did serve to raise awareness of concerns about the competence-based approach and how it is being implemented.

On more detailed issues, for example concerning functional analysis, there has been disagreement between Stewart and Hamlin (1992a, pp21-32) and Mansfield (1993, pp19-22). The association of the NCVQ approach to assessment with functionalism and behaviourism has been criticised by Marshall (1991, pp56-64) who suggests that this model of competence-based assessment may be inappropriate except, perhaps, at basic levels. Winter (1992, pp100-115) argues that much criticism of competence-based education is more justifiable as a critique of the particular format in which it is currently presented than of its underlying principles.

Support for competence-based education is expressed by Raggatt (1991, pp61-80) but he combines this with criticism of the NVQ approach. In considering work-based assessment Boffy (1990, pp182-200) regards a competence-based system of qualifications (such as that proposed by NCVQ) as helping to alleviate some of the problems in this area. It is easy to criticise existing approaches to teaching, learning and assessment but Stewart and Hamlin (1992b, pp9-16) warn against exaggerating the weaknesses of these and so assuming that competence-based education is the sole remedy. They note that, in almost all subjects, whether academic, professional or vocational, examinations are not the only means of assessment. Similarly, nearly all higher education institutions have policies to increase access and, without embracing competence-based approaches, have had considerable success in doing this.

Competence-based approaches originated with programmes of preparation for particular occupations, such as teaching, in the USA, and were later adopted by the NCVQ (Tuxworth, 1989, pp10-25). Thus 'Competency-Based Vocational Education' (CBVE) became a standard approach. Before there has been time to evaluate its success in preparing people for particular occupations, the approach is being extended into more general education (eg, General National Vocational Qualifications - GNVQs) and into higher education (eg, in many modular programmes). Plans to bring NVQs into higher levels of education, including degree work, have met some resistance (Sanders and Tysome, 1991; Nash, 1992). It has been noted that the 'logic of modularisation' in higher education requires large scale implementation across a range of subjects, academic and vocational (Brady, 1992, pp34-39); this provides a means by which the competence-based approach is spread. Thus we are faced with both an approach to curriculum organisation and assessment and an approach to stating curriculum intentions which are inter-related and controversial, yet which are already dominant landmarks on the current educational scene in the UK.

3

The concept of competence

Few would dispute that there is a need to provide a high quality, more comprehensive and more extensive education for those who leave school at 16 or 18 and do not enter higher education. Another proposition which attracts widespread agreement is that what has been on offer for this large group of young people is in many ways neither what they nor potential employers need. A plethora of qualifications of variable status, significance and worth cannot be desirable. Unfavourable comparisons with the education of this age group in Europe have been made (Guy, 1991, pp47-60).

Recognition of these problems led to the setting up by the government of the NCVQ in 1986. This official body established a new pattern of vocational qualifications which enshrined competency-based vocational education. The original intentions of NCVQ were that NVQs should be systems for accrediting learning (Hyland, 1993a, pp5-7) rather than learning programmes in their own right. However, due to the 'hegemonic influence which the NCVQ has managed to achieve since its establishment in 1986' (Hyland, 1992a, pp29-36) there is pressure on examining bodies and local curriculum planners to conform to a particular competence-based approach.

That people performing a job should be competent is an attractive and apparently 'commonsense' idea. However, on closer examination both the attractive and commonsense aspects of the approach appear to be rather superficial. A major problem, for example, is a certain lack of agreement concerning the nature of competence (UDACE, 1989, pp1-33) and its implementation (Haffenden and Brown, 1989, pp132-170). While the stress may be on outcomes in that 'competence is concerned with what people can do rather than with what they know' (UDACE, 1989, pp1-12), it may also be on a somewhat broader 'possession and development of sufficient skills, knowledge, appropriate attitudes and experience for successful performance in life roles' (FEU, 1984).

Jessup (1991, pp6-39) likewise has suggested two approaches to defining competence. While it might refer to a specific set of skills necessary to carry out a particular job, it could also include the qualities necessary to perform a wider occupational role. If the second, broader concept is used then it is important that assessment procedures reflect this. An emphasis on outcome behaviours will surely inhibit this.

A not unreasonable conclusion from the considerable literature on competence-based approaches would be that the only agreement is that it is undesirable to have in employment people who are incompetent! 'Everybody is for standards and everyone is against incompetence' (Norris, 1991, p331). An indication of the problems associated with the concept of competence is that the word and its derivatives are used in a variety of ways. People can be 'competent' either in general or with regard to their performance in an occupation or in a particular job. However, we also describe performances as 'competent'.

At first sight the idea of occupational competence expressed in terms of statements of what a person 'can do' appears very attractive to those charged with the responsibility of designing vocational curricula and particularly for those concerned with assessing student performance. Surely people simply need to possess the necessary skills to perform a particular task. If they fail to come up to this standard they should not be appointed to the job, however hard they may have worked on a course, or for however long they may have studied.

> Common usage licenses talk not only of competence with respect to a performance in general but also of individual *competences* which that performance can exhibit. (Carr, 1993, p254)

This emphasis on individual competences has been criticised by Ashworth (1992, pp8-17) who draws a distinction between 'having NCVQ competences' and actually being competent. He emphasises the importance of knowledge and understanding and goes on to stress the need for people to engage fully in teamwork, something which is not promoted by the NCVQ emphasis on personal competences. Hodkinson (1992, pp30-39) suggests two possible models of competence, the behaviouristic and the interactive. The NCVQ approach is seen as emphasising the former. In other words not only has there been a rather hasty introduction of competence-based education, but also the introduction of a particular version of it.

In practice, we do not always use the word competent in an absolute sense (ie, to indicate 'can do' as opposed to 'cannot do'). In everyday speech we use expressions such as: 'She is a highly competent person'; 'he is fairly competent'; 'she is rather incompetent'; 'he is totally incompetent'. Thus we frequently think in terms of degrees of competence. If this is so, are we any further forward in assessing people's suitability for particular jobs than by relying on traditional qualifications? Appeals to down-to-earth commonsense may make the idea of competence initially attractive, but further reflection soon reveals an element of confusion.

Stewart and Hamlin (1993, pp3-9) have noted that there is a problem with using 'competent' to mean that a person is fully competent in all aspects of a job. They suggest it would be more helpful if a notion of 'competence potential' or 'threshold competence' were used. This would accord with the view that overall competence is the result of experience and training, rather than an outcome to be demonstrated.

If the concept of competence is problematic then so is its assessment. However, it could be argued that the assessment problems can be overcome, or at least alleviated, and so it would be unwise to reject the idea of competence-based education solely because of drawbacks in the assessment procedures in schemes such as NVQs. Hamlin and Stewart (1994, pp13-17) are sympathetic towards competence-based qualifications but they have drawn attention to problems of assessment of competence, particularly at the higher levels of NVQs.

Competence and knowledge

The debate concerning the desirability or otherwise of competence-based education to some extent reflects earlier debates concerning the relative importance of 'theory' and 'practical work' in technical and vocational education. It is easy to ridicule the writing of essays on 'How I would mend a bicycle puncture' but 'theory' in this situation can be seen as a reservoir of knowledge (information) and understanding (insight) which can be applied in different situations. One danger of competence-based education (or at least of some versions of it) is that competence is interpreted (and therefore assessed) in terms of outcomes. This leads to problems concerning when, and how often, these outcomes are assessed and interpreted as evidence of competence. Atkins et al (1993, p7) note that there is no standard definition of competence-based assessment. In their report they use it to mean 'the assessment of the acceptability of the performance of a defined activity against predetermined standards of criteria. The activity can require intellectual, personal or practical achievements.'

It can be argued that if a person can demonstrate 'competence' then they must have the necessary underpinning knowledge. This is the assumption made by those who insist on the demonstration of behavioural outcomes. Such an approach reduces the significance and importance of knowledge. Hyland (1992b, pp7-12) observes that 'there is something unsatisfactory about a theoretical perspective which apparently recognises knowledge and understanding only to the extent that these are revealed in the performance of occupational tasks'. In the development of GNVQs there has been a greater recognition of the importance of knowledge and of its separate assessment. However, the emphasis tends to be on the information recall aspect of knowledge as it relates to particular occupations.

It is a gross mutation of the aims of education to suggest either that knowledge is only important to the extent that it reveals itself in the performance of certain tasks or that the only understanding worth having is that which contributes to vocational competence. (Hyland, 1990, p19)

It is the question of the amount and nature of the knowledge which underpins competence which has proved to be one of the most controversial areas in the introduction of NVQs. Critics of CBVE (Hyland, 1993b, pp57-68; Smithers, 1993) have alleged that knowledge is neglected in the approach; underpinning knowledge and theory are not tested separately but inferred. In its reply to the Smithers Report, the NCVQ (1993) insists that NVQs 'unequivocally require the separate assessment of knowledge where this is necessary to confirm competence'. NCVQ was particularly stung by, as it saw the situation, criticism that if knowledge is not imparted through instruction, syllabuses and courses which are fully prescribed as part of the qualifications, it cannot be properly gained.

This is perhaps the nub of the dispute between supporters and opponents of NVQs. Despite their protestations in reply to Smithers, NCVQ and its supporters do seem reluctant to allow much importance to be given to knowledge, and certainly to any separate teaching or assessment of that knowledge. While Stewart and Hamlin (1993, pp3-9) see an increasingly important role for the demonstration of underpinning knowledge, understanding and skills as NVQ levels are ascended, Moran (1991, pp8-9) typifies those supporters of CBVE who are reluctant to make many concessions in this direction when he writes 'even in the most professional occupations the proportion of 'knowledge-heavy' competences is quite few'. He adds later 'whilst knowledge is a proper and legitimate element of any competence it should not be given undue deference'.

Wolf (1989) discusses the question 'Can competence and knowledge mix?' To ask such a question is to go against the theory of NVQ which appears to assume that knowledge and competence are so closely linked that demonstration of a competence necessarily involves possession of any requisite knowledge. She writes:

I hope to show that there is no bifurcation between competence and education. The approach is perfectly compatible with the learning of higher level skills, the acquisition of generalisable knowledge (and understanding) and with broad-based courses. (Wolf, 1989, p39)

Approaching the problem from a different perspective Hyland (1991, p7) writes:

It is quite wrong to construct an opposition between competence-based qualifications and knowledge-based ones as if they were dealing with radically different phenomena.

There is a danger that the competence-based approach, with its downgrading of knowledge at the expense of action, further exacerbates the academic-vocational divide. A robot 'can do'; human beings can and should reflect on what to do, how and when to do it and above all they should reflect on why they are doing it. In the UK practical activities tend to be held in low esteem. Is this why competence-based approaches to vocational education have been emphasised? There is an assumption that many jobs do not require much knowledge or thinking; that can be left to managers of one sort or another.

It will be pointed out that competence-based approaches figure prominently in many non-technical areas such as management itself. Competence has been seen as a basic curriculum dimension, along with relevance and flexibility (FEU, 1981). Here again, we have two attractive terms in that nobody wants curricula that are irrelevant or lead to inflexibility. But, like competence, the terms relevance and flexibility involve concepts which require clarification. Only then can we explore their relationship with competence. This is a complex area which leads us back to the question of underpinning knowledge.

Fleming (1991, pp9-12) has proposed the term 'meta-competence' to describe a reflective awareness of existing competence. He regards this meta-competence, which is particularly important in higher education, as highlighting competences which work on other competences. This is an interesting idea which moves us away from the behaviouristic approach associated with much competence-based education.

Historical perspective - stating curriculum intentions

A major problem in curriculum design in any education or training with an occupational focus (even if long-term) concerns expressing curriculum intentions in a way that is helpful to student, teacher and potential employer. At one time, at least for some curriculum planners, the behavioural objectives approach seemed to be the answer. Experience and reflection soon found flaws in this approach (see, for example, Wesson (1983a) pp51-58, and Wesson (1983b) pp75-79). Is there now a danger that, in a desire for precision and comprehension, we may be embracing in competence-based education an approach which is similarly flawed and limited?

The behavioural objectives approach is often traced back to

developments in the United States in the early part of this century. However, problems with expressing curriculum intentions solely in the form of lists of subject-matter content had been noted earlier than this. In the UK, some syllabi of the Science and Art Department had attempted to be more precise. For example, an experimental physics syllabus includes statements such as:

> He ought to calculate the length of sonorous waves. He ought to be able to describe and illustrate the condition of a vibrating string or column of air at its nodal points. He ought to be able to determine the positions of the foci of spherical mirrors, both concave and convex. He ought to be able to compare accurately the strength of one magnet with that of another. (Science and Art Department, 1862, p34)

A feature common to statements like the above syllabus, the behavioural objectives which permeated curricula in this country in the 1960s and 1970s, and the present competence-based curricula is that they make assessment easier. Perhaps it would be preferable to say that they make certain aspects of assessment easier. While assessment is important in education there is a danger of ending up with assessment-dominated curricula. What is needed is a means of stating curriculum intentions which does justice to the nature of the learning process and to the particular subject-matter.

Supporters of the behavioural objectives approach did make use of Bloom's taxonomy to develop objectives relating to other than basic psychomotor skills. However, problems were encountered in attempting to deal with 'higher levels' of learning in this way and in dealing with the 'affective domain'. In a rather similar way users of the competence approach have recognised that in doing many jobs, perhaps all jobs, appropriate attitudes are important. Thus competencies are sometimes assumed to include attitudes as well as skills, although this certainly presents problems if the emphasis is solely or largely on outcomes. The FEU has promoted the idea of 'moral competence' (Wright, 1989). Competence statements for areas of work such as educational guidance for adults have been prepared (Oakeshott, 1991). Linking the idea of competence-based education with professional, managerial and human service occupations may be difficult but it has been attempted through the identification of so-called 'soft skill competencies' (Spencer, 1983). These are elucidated through procedures such as functional analysis, leading to criticism from some writers (Marshall, 1991, pp56-64; Stewart and Hamlin, 1992a, pp21-32). On the other hand it is claimed that the 'Job Competence Assessment process' 'permits description, in very specific behavioural terms, not only of the elements of a job but the characteristics and skills of the persons who do the job well' (Spencer, 1983, p18).

The development of the NVQ approach places emphasis on the end results of learning and experience, that is on outcomes.

> Most people recognise that NVQs are competence-based but the concept is open to a number of interpretations. What is distinctive about an NVQ is that the specification of competence is explicitly defined. The competence statements... identify the focus of desired achievement not how one might decide whether or not an individual's performance is satisfactory. (Darby, 1992, pp17-28)

Hall and Jones (1976, p29) see competency statements as an intermediate stage between statements of general goals (few needed) and specific objectives (many needed). However, inasmuch as competency statements are expressed in terms of outcomes, the problems remain. Ramsay (1993, pp70-89) maintains that competencies cannot but be tainted with the behaviourism of the objectives movement.

> In the UK, Behaviourism's most notable recent conquest began a few years ago with NCVQ's decision to employ it as the sole means of transforming Vocational Training. Learning Objectives were rewritten in terms of 'objectively' definable and observable behaviour, re-named 'Competences', coupled with the idea of student-centred learning and unleashed on an, apparently, totally unprepared body of academics in all walks of further and higher education life.

The writer thus typifies those who see competencies as behavioural objectives resurrected in a possibly more subtle and insidious form.

What sort of competence?

One of the problems with competence is whether it is a personality characteristic (possibly demonstrated by certain behaviours) or whether it is a series of outcomes (often described as competencies).

> In particular it is not clear whether competence is a personal attribute, an act or the outcome of an action; moreover the idea of competence, as currently used, is open to complaints that it is atomistic, individualistic and unable to cover all types of relevant behaviour or mental activity. (Ashworth and Saxton, 1990, p3)

In NVQ programmes the emphasis on work-based assessment appears to favour the outcomes approach which, while perhaps making assessment easier, can become very mechanistic.

Writing about educational, psychological and measurement issues relating to the competence-performance distinction, Wood and Power (1987, p409) observed: 'There was competence as enhanced performance and competence as the deep structure responsible for the surface performance'. We have to decide whether a competent person is one who does perform certain tasks in a certain (pre-determined) way or a person who has the ability and willingness to perform those tasks as and when necessary.

There are those who consider that competence-based approaches need not be reductionist. Everard (1993, pp19-21) does not see the competence approach as a mechanistic assessment-led approach. He claims that the reflective-practitioner approach can be built into the competence-based approach. There is evidence that some advocates of competence-based approaches do recognise the importance of students acquiring more than just job-related skills. 'Moral competence' is seen as a dimension of all other forms of competence (Wright, 1989). However, this view could be seen as reducing morality to a behaviouristic level.

Competence, employment and education

Certain drawbacks of the competence-based approach in terms of knowledge, functionalism and behaviourism have been noted. These can be related to occupational performance. However, underlying these is a more fundamental problem. CBVE concentrates on preparation for work; it would appear to contradict the idea of a liberal education. While some writers may discuss personal and generic competencies, competence-based education tends to merge into CBVE, thus reflecting a utilitarian view of the educational enterprise at all levels. Beyond this, CBVE concentrates on particular jobs, thus reinforcing its narrowing effect. It may serve to satisfy some particular industrial or other employment needs now but it may easily become another aspect of 'short-termism'.

Concentration on what a person can do now is a narrow approach even in terms of employment. Among other things people need to be prepared for a working life extending over several decades. It is now becoming recognised that continuing education and training will be required to support this. It is not possible to predict employment requirements in the detail assumed by a competence-based approach. A frequently stated truism is that we live in a period of rapid technological change. Curriculum planners have the difficult task of taking account of this but the narrowing effect of CBVE may inhibit this. Once again the question of 'underpinning knowledge' is raised.

Rassekh (1985, pp51-55), in looking towards the future, listed some major problems and suggested a number of solutions. Among these were schemes for intermittent education such as part-study, part-work arrangements and more emphasis on education for an occupation, but he also noted needs for constant updating of the scientific content of education and for the introduction of an overall, interdisciplinary, problem-centred approach.

A sound knowledge base is essential to professional and technical performance at any level above the most mechanical and dehumanising assembly-line factory work. Separation of competence from knowledge, and technical knowledge from more basic 'academic' knowledge is misleading. The history of Mechanics' Institutes in the last century showed this when attempts to introduce technical and vocational education often floundered because potential students were lacking in basic, general education (Hole, 1853).

Competence, education and experience

The introduction of GNVQs, particularly into schools, raises serious issues regarding the vocationalisation of education. There is a danger that it reflects a utilitarianism which neglects broader aspects of education.

For much of our educational history, and at various levels, education has been seen in terms of overlapping concepts such as development, character building, experience and socialisation. These concepts have emerged from various different ideologies but the underlying common assumption is that certain qualities, of educational value, can only be acquired through a sustained and lengthy experience of education involving encounters with teachers and with fellow students. Some might regard that typically English institution, the boarding school, as taking the idea too far; however, in higher education, despite the recent rapid expansion, residence remains important for many students. Newman (1852, pp122-124) preferred 'residence and tutorial superintendence' to 'professors and examinations'. Now, with competency-based education, we have a strong emphasis on outcomes which logically diminishes or removes attendance requirements. While this might be welcomed by those who see education as an oppressive form of social control, it has serious implications for the conduct and expectations of both part-time and full-time education.

It might be argued that developments in flexible learning which have helped to expand educational opportunities have also struck a blow against the idea of residence and community as essential aspects of education. However, the Open University, one of the UK's more successful recent educational innovations, does have regular tutorial classes, summer schools and telephone tutorials which attempt to provide the mutual support and exchange of ideas which are characteristic of traditional education, whether vocational or academic. Furthermore the use of set texts as well as packaged materials further emphasises that processes as well as products are important.

Equally, the idea of 'formation' cannot be neglected. Its results may be impossible to predict or define but we should not too readily abandon an idea that has permeated education for a long time. Association with teachers (directly or indirectly), and with other students, over an extended period of time, is desirable to enable a student to 'internalise' any subject.

Similarly, Squires (1987, p121) suggests that there is a need for the learner to have practical skills 'confirmed (practised and overlearned)' rather than just acquired. In the past, vocational education may have involved, through the apprenticeship system, overlong periods of occupational preparation. This does not invalidate the need for educational experience. The emphasis in competence-based education on outcomes does justice neither to curriculum content nor curriculum processes.

As Hyland (1993b, pp57-68) has noted, competence-based education makes an artificial distinction between thinking and doing. This division has bedevilled education in the past; we should be seeking ways of diminishing it not extending it.

Over 20 years ago, a principal of a technical college wrote:

> Human beings are not blocks of timber, stone or metal, are not equally imprinted by the same studies, and technical instruction needs much thoughtful analysis before its total educational effect on any one individual can be accurately assessed. (Warren, 1972, p1)

This advice has largely gone unheeded. The behavioural objectives approach and, even more, the current competence-based approaches have tended to make vocational education more mechanical and instrumental, serving neither the student's individual nor social needs. In the long term this will benefit neither employers nor the community at large. Taking a long-term view one can argue that a broader education benefits not only the individual but also society. When discussing the nature of a university education, Newman (1852, pp122-124) argued that 'the useful is not always good, the good is always useful'. He goes on to discuss what he means by 'good' and 'useful' as he attempts to counter the crude utilitarianism of his age. For our purposes it is sufficient to note this expression of the idea that benefit to society will come from education in a liberal sense rather than from an over-emphasis on training for particular jobs.

In a similar vein, the author of a 'Handbook of Mechanics Institutes' wrote:

> A boorishness of manner, and a scarcely concealed contempt for literary pursuits, may be sometimes observed among the most diligent and successful students in the sciences at Mechanics' Institutes. Such a mistaken depreciation of the amenities of literature must in many ways interfere with their opportunities for applying their scientific knowledge to advantage, either as regards themselves or society. (Traice, 1863, p12)

There is starting to emerge some evidence that supporters of a competence-based approach are taking account of criticisms concerning the narrowness of the approach, particularly with regard to assessment issues. Wolf (1994, pp3-6) writes:

> A common criticism of competence-based qualifications is that they imply a 'mechanistic and atomistic' approach to learning and assessment. This is, of course, quite at odds with the purpose of a competence-based system, but the process of defining standards, and expressing competence in terms of outcomes, means that what is integrated in reality is often disaggregated in the assessment specification.

A comparison of GNVQs with NVQs suggests that this assessment issue is being reviewed.

Conclusion

Why has there been comparatively little resistance to the advent of competency-based education? One obvious answer is that it has been imposed by government, through the activities of bodies such as the NCVQ. A second reason may be suggested. Competence-based education is 'anti-traditional' in terms of content and method. It tends to downgrade knowledge and teacher-planned learning and to stress outcomes and student-centred approaches. Certainly curriculum process is important, but so is the content. It is misleading to separate them. 'Learning how to learn' is essential but it must be associated with learning valid content. As Jonathan (1987, p166) says:

> Insight that the learning process is itself important is replaced by the false claim that it is all-important: learning skills are no longer seen as a means of

applying and extending knowledge; they are offered as a replacement of it.

Consequently an approach to education which embraces a narrow utilitarianism can be advocated using 'progressive' jargon. There is a danger that the problems and contradictions may be ignored. For example, in recent years in colleges (and to some extent in schools) there has been considerable emphasis on education as experience and on associated ideas such as group interaction. Competence-based education, with its emphasis on outcomes, switches attention back from processes to products.

While society needs to place a greater value on practical activities (and on occupations concerned with making and maintaining things) teachers need to be less apologetic about 'academic' studies. In particular, academic studies should not be seen as separate from practical activities, nor should it be assumed that academic studies are only suitable for particular types of student. The current emphasis on student-centred approaches has perhaps gone too far in stressing individual and short-term interests. A broader view of all education is required. Such education (for all) should embrace the academic and vocational, theory and practice, personal development and social awareness. Should it not also include ethical and aesthetic awareness? Of course, it is easy to say that this should be so; it is an enormous and difficult task for curriculum planners to achieve an appropriate balance in all areas of education. However, it may be preferable to expend energy on this task rather than on working on the specification of behavioural outcomes within what is really an arbitrary framework.

Perhaps the only way to ensure that people really can do the various tasks required in employment is to make available to everyone, initial and continuing education which does justice to human nature and to subject matter. A problem with NVQs and other forms of competence-based education is that they tend to oversimplify both. Apparently easier assessment or possibly more effective management should not be allowed to push us into taking short cuts in curriculum planning.

Bibliography

Ashworth, P.D. (1992), *Being competent and having competencies*, Journal of Further and Higher Education, 16 (3) 8-17.

Ashworth, P.D. and Saxton, J. (1990), *On Competence*, Journal of Further and Higher Education, 14 (2) 3-25.

Atkins, M.J., Beattie, J and Dockrell, W.B. (1993), *Assessment Issues in Higher Education*, Department of Employment.

Boffy, R. (1990), *Occupational competence and work-based learning: the future for FE?* in Bees, M. and Swords, M. (eds) 'National Vocational Qualifications and Further Education', Kogan Page, p182-200.

Brady, D. (1992), *Taking it to bits: some problems of modularisation*, NAVET Papers, VII, 34-39.

Carr, D. (1993), *Questions of Competence*, British Journal of Educational Studies, XXXI, (3), 253-271.

Darby, M. (1992), *An NCVQ Update*, NASD Journal, (26), 17-28.

Everard, K.B. (1993), *Values and the Competence Approach*, NAVET Papers, IX, 19-21.

Fennell, E. (1990), Editorial in Competence and Assessment, (10), p2.

FEU (1981), *Relevance, Flexibility and Competence*.

FEU (1984), *Towards a Competency-based System*.

Finch, C.R. and Crunkilton, J.R. (1989), *Competence-based Education*, in Curriculum Development in Vocational and Technical Education. New York: Allyn and Bacon (3rd edition).

Fleming, D. (1991), *The Concept of Meta-competence*, Competence and Assessment, (16), 9-12.

Guy, R. (1991), *Serving the Needs of Industry?*, in Raggatt, P. and Unwin, L. (eds) 'Change and Intervention: Vocational Education and Training', Falmer Press.

Haffenden, I. and Brown, A. (1989), *Towards the implementation of competence-based curricula in Colleges of Further Education*, in Burke, J.W. 'Competence-based Education and Training', Falmer Press.

Hall, G.E. and Jones, H.L. (1976), *Competency-based Education: a process for the improvement of education*, New Jersey: Prentice Hall.

Hamlin, B. and Stewart, J. (1994), *Competence-based Qualifications: monitoring forward momentum*, Competence and Assessment (24), 13-17.

Hodkinson, P. (1992), *Alternative models of competence in vocational education and training*, Journal of Further and Higher Education, 16 (2), 30-39.

Hole, J. (1853), *An Essay on the History and Management of Literary, Scientific and Mechanics' Institutes*, Longmans.

Hyland, T. (1990), *Education, Vocationalism and Competence*, Forum, 33 (1), 18-19.

Hyland, T. (1991), *Knowledge, performance and competence-based assessment*, Educa 118, 7.

Hyland, T. (1992a), *NVQs and the reform of Vocational Education and Training*, NASD Journal, (26), 29-36.

Hyland, T. (1992b), *The vicissitudes of adult education: competence, epistemology and reflective practice*, Education Today, 42 (2), 7-12.

Hyland, T. (1993a), *Outcomes and Competence in Higher Education*, Educational Change and Development, 13 (2), 5-7.

Hyland, T. (1993b), *Competence, Knowledge and Education*, Journal of Philosophy of Education, 27 (1), 57-68.

Jessup, G. (1991), *Statements of Competence and Standards*, in 'Outcomes: NVQs and the emerging world of education and training', Falmer Press.

Jonathan, R. (1987), *The Youth Training Scheme and Core Skills: an educational analysis*, in Holt, M. (ed) 'Skills and Vocationalism: the easy answer', Milton Keynes: Open University Press.

Mansfield, B. (1993), *Competence-based Qualifications: a response*, Journal of European Industrial Training, 17 (3), 19-22.

Marshall, K. (1991), *NVQs: an assessment of the 'Outcomes' approach to Education and Training*, Journal of Further and Higher Education, 15 (3), 56-64.

Moran, D. (1991), *The role of knowledge in competence-based measurement*, Educa (September) (115), 8-9.

Nash, I. (1992), *Dispute on rigid skills formula*, Times Educational Supplement, 29th May, p4.

NCVQ (1993), *A statement on 'All our futures - Britain's Education Revolution'*.

Newman, Cardinal, J.H. (1852), *The Idea of a University*, San Francisco: Rinehart Press (1960 edition).

Norris, N. (1991), *The trouble with competence*, Cambridge Journal of Education, 21 (3), 331-341.

Oakeshott, M. (1991), *Educational Guidance for Adults: identifying competences*, FEU and UDACE.

Raggatt, P. (1991), *Quality Assurance and NVQs*, in Raggatt, P. and Unwin, L. 'Change and Innovation: Vocational Education and Training', Falmer Press.

Ramsay, J. (1993), *The Hybrid Course: Competences and Behaviourism in Higher Education*, Journal of Further and Higher Education, 17 (3). 70-89.

Rassekh, S. (1985), *Reforms in education today and the challenge of tomorrow* in 'Reflections on the future development of education', Paris: UNESCO.

Sanders, C. and Tysome, T. (1991), *V-Cs balk at new qualifications*, Times Higher Education Supplement, 29th November, p3.

Science and Art Department (1862), *Experimental Physics Syllabus*.

Smithers, A. (1993), *All our futures: Britain's Education Revolution*, Channel 4 Television.

Spencer, L.M. (1983), *Soft skill competencies*, Edinburgh: SCRE.

Squires, G. (1987), *The Curriculum Beyond School*, Hodder and Stoughton.

Stewart, J. and Hamlin, B. (1992a), *Competence-based qualifications: the case against change*, Journal of European Industrial Training, 16 (7), 21-32.

Stewart, J. and Hamlin, B. (1992b), *Competence-based qualifications: the case for established methodologies*, Journal of European Industrial Training, 16 (10), 9-16.

Stewart, J. and Hamlin, B. (1993), *Competence-based qualifications: a way forward*, Journal of European Industrial Training, 17 (6), 3-9.

Traice, W.H.J. (1863), *Handbook of Mechanics' Institutes*, Longmans (2nd edition).

Tuxworth, E. (1989), *Competence-based education and training: background and origins*, in Burke 'Competence-based education and training', Falmer Press, pp10-25.

UDACE (1989), *Understanding Competence*, Leicester: National Institute of Adult Continuing Education, pp1-33.

Warren, H. (1972), *A Philosophy of Technical Education*, Association of Colleges for Further and Higher Education.

Wesson, A. (1983a), *Behaviourally Defined Objectives: a critique*, Part I, Vocational Aspect of Education XXXV, (91), 51-58.

Wesson, A. (1983b), *Behaviourally Defined Objectives: a critique*, Part II, Vocational Aspect XXXV, (92), 75-79.

Winter, R. (1992), *'Quality Management' or 'Educative Workplace': alternative versions of competence-based education*, Journal of Further and Higher Education, 16 (3), 100-115.

Wolf, A. (1989), *Can Competence and Knowledge Mix?*, in Burke 'Competence-based education and training', Falmer Press.

Wolf, A. (1994), *Assessing the broad skills within occupational competence*, Competence and Assessment, (25), 3-6.

Wood, R. and Power (1987), *Aspects of the competence-performance distinction: education, psychological and measurement issues*, Journal of Curriculum Studies, 19 (5), 409-424.

Wright, D. (1989), *Moral Competence: an exploration of the role of moral education in further education*, FEU.

2 Achieving consistency in NVQ assessment

Christine Johnson

Abstract

This paper summarises the findings of an investigation into the level of consistency achieved when judging evidence of NVQ competences. A micro-study of procedures involved and outcomes awarded by a team of six staff carrying out the accreditation of evidence for two competence statements in the Business Administration Level III Course was undertaken. It was found that, despite areas of compatibility in the procedures adopted, the outcomes awarded by staff and the reasons given for the award or non-award of 'competence' varied quite considerably. Despite the use of experienced and qualified assessors, problems were identified when assessment took place in a criterion-referenced context. Issues raised included the wording and terminology used by Lead Bodies, which were felt to be prone to misinterpretation; and concern was expressed about the amount of time which would be required to carry out effective future internal verification.

Introduction

There is now a greater acceptance that education and training programmes should concentrate upon outcomes as well as inputs. Competence and quality are interrelated themes, in terms of both teaching and learning, demanding analysis of needs, good design, accreditation, progression and negotiated entitlement. Jessup (1991), for example, stresses that competence should not be referred to as a 'low or minimum level of performance'. He likens competence to the 'standards required successfully to perform an activity or function', reiterating that there is no place for 'second best'.

Such issues about quality and excellence and what this means in a competence-based system of education and training require further investigation. After all, in a norm-referenced system, with an acceptance of the many inadequacies it possessed, there were strengths in the provision of a crude guide to quality, such as a supposition that those who had passed an examination represented some form of elite group. It would also appear that employers still use grades achieved at GCSE and 'A' level performance as a strong indicator for recruitment of potential employees.

In assessing NVQs on the other hand, there should be no comparison between one person and the next, as competence is defined as the ability to meet the performance standards consolidated by the performance criteria. The criterion-referenced NCVQ assessment is therefore a completely different form of assessment for lecturers, who have now to move from assessing in a conventional norm-referenced manner with varying degrees of excellence to two categories of either 'competent' or 'not yet competent'. There is no scope for mediocrity or excellence; the candidate must simply meet the standards specified for the units in which they are being assessed at a given point in time. To date however, little attention has been devoted to criterion-referenced assessment in the context of NVQs.

Nonetheless, in a market-led culture it would be foolish to ignore the fact that higher education establishments and employers will still seek to recruit the 'best'. Failing this, an overall acceptable quality in, eg, assessment (the concern of this paper) is vital and, in order to achieve this, it is important that the standards are understood by all who use them.

The fact that the standards are described in written form in itself causes an abundance of problems. For example, if the description is too wordy then this may overwhelm the user. Equally problematic is the use of too few words in the description, which could result in misinterpretation. Additionally, a competence-based system of education and training needs to address the relationship between the Lead Body's definition of 'competence' and the assessor's perception of 'competent'. It is possible when making judgements about human activities to feel 'absolutely certain' that an individual can do something and on other occasions we may be 'fairly sure' or perhaps 'uncertain' about individuals' capabilities. Alternatively we may be 'absolutely sure' that they are unable to perform the activity. The one thing that we can be absolutely sure of is that we can never be totally certain of accuracy when making judgements about human activities.

There is some relevant work on this topic. Reports which have been produced by NCVQ and the Employment Department (Jessup (1991) and Mitchell and Cuthbert (1989)) focus on examples of good practice and procedure which were simply aimed at helping ensure quality of assessment, though, less reassuringly, Johnson and Blinkhorn (1992) found that NVQ practitioners held many views concerning quality criteria some of which were shared but few of which had been developed systematically.

One problem is that it is doubtful whether the performance element can be examined in isolation from the underpinning knowledge and understanding required. For example to deal with visitors at a reception area will require many skills including social interaction, knowledge of company procedures, tact, discretion and knowledge of how to deal with callers possessing different personalities and with a wide variety of needs. Indeed, Maclure (1991) questions the advisability of placing barriers between performance-linked and other types of knowledge and understanding, and this is evident by the emphasis now being placed upon a general vocational competence such as General Vocational Qualifications (GNVQs). Such considerations cannot help but call into question assessment based purely on observation, as Wolf's work (1991) suggests.

There have also been difficulties experienced by both students and staff in the interpretation of range statements and performance criteria for units of competence. It is interesting to note that included in the criteria for Assessor Awards in the National Standards for Assessment and Verification (1992) is the requirement that the assessor produce evidence as follows:

> difficulties in interpreting performance criteria are referred promptly and accurately to an appropriate authority

It would appear that there is an acceptance that there may well be difficulties in interpretation!

Certainly, Mitchell and Sturton (1993), when investigating the candidate's role in assessment, found that there were a number of inconsistencies and misinterpretations both in guidance literature and current practice. They found that there was considerable concern from candidates with regard to issues in respect of evidence collection, suitability of evidence, matching of evidence with standards and knowing if the evidence was sufficient and of the appropriate quality. These issues were also found to be problematic for assessors and awarding bodies and it was stressed by the researchers that urgent development work was required to address these issues.

Gealy (1993), discussing feedback on the development of NVQs and SVQs at higher levels, drew attention to the variety of ways in which one of the criteria had been interpreted by participants. The interpretations ranged from a requirement for the assessor to watch each candidate carrying out and gathering performance evidence for each element to using whatever assessment methods were judged relevant. It appeared that there may be misinterpretation and that national guidance should take heed of this need for clarification. Thus, it would appear that although there has been some limited research carried out in the area of consistency of assessment in NVQs, concern has been expressed, where it has taken place, about the reliability of the process. There thus appeared to be considerable justification for collecting additional evidence to examine this issue.

True, NCVQ has published guidelines on the nature of the evidence required (NCVQ 1991) and additional information exists in the form of performance criteria and range statements for each of the elements of competence. The interpretation of these guidelines is crucial, however, if an evaluation of current practice is to be carried out. At the same time, Hallmark and Horton (1991) and Wolf (1988), whilst producing reports outlining models, offer little guidance on the interpretation of checking the acceptability of an NVQ assessment of competence. A need exists to capture the quality of sound assessment and identify bad practice at the point of assessment.

As a result of the above, while it is normally assumed that if staff carry out Assessor Training and achieve a recognised Lead Body Award this should equip them for carrying out NVQ assessment of competence, it was felt by the author that it would be useful to examine the interpretations of staff who had carried out Assessor Training to establish if there was consistency in the evidence which they accepted as 'competent' or 'not yet competent'. Hence, the aims of this study were to gain a clearer understanding of the assessment procedures adopted by trained assessors who carry out accreditation of evidence presented by students. An exploration of the issues involved and the highlighting of any difficulties found in the standardisation of assessment would be the best means of ensuring future 'quality and consistency' of assessment in NVQ programmes.

Course details

The NVQ Business Administration Level III Course chosen for the study was delivered by full-time lecturers all of whom had been involved for a minimum of two years with NVQ and in some cases included staff who had participated in the pilot scheme.

The students were following an NVQ Level III full-time course of study offered as a two-year course (APL can reduce the time). Students are encouraged to negotiate their programmes of study and APL is actively encouraged with reference to the availability of this mode of accreditation on every course document or learning package. Students with prior knowledge or experience are able to accelerate through the programme at their own pace.

Staff found that students had experienced difficulty in coming to terms with the requirements of a competence-based philosophy. Whilst staff have given greater attention to showing students how to build up portfolio evidence and produced a video showing an accreditation session, this area still presents some students with difficulties.

Methodology and data analysis

The methodology adopted in the study included collecting data which would be used by students as evidence for two competence statements in the unit of Reception required in the NVQ Business Administration Level III course. The staff and students were assured of anonymity. The data was collected from six students, including students from a wide range of ages, with educational backgrounds ranging from no qualifications to Higher National level and one student who was claiming accreditation of prior learning for the Reception Unit.

The research investigation included taped non-directive interviews with six members of staff to establish the procedures they adopted when carrying out accreditation of evidence presented by students and to highlight any difficulties found in achieving consistency of assessment.

The interviewees were then asked to outline the accreditation procedure they adopted when reviewing evidence. On completion of this they were again played the tape, which stated that they would be given two competence statements in the Reception Unit namely:

3.1.1   visitors are received courteously, and their identity is established
3.1.6   non-routine and emergency demands are dealt with promptly and effectively

Six students had presented portfolios of evidence for these two competence statements which they would be asked to review as 'competent' or 'not yet competent'. All interviewees, it was stressed, would be given the same evidence and the need for confidentiality concerning their views was vital.

There then took place a description of the procedure which was adopted at an accreditation session followed by a review of the evidence provided by six NVQ Level III Business Administration students for the Reception Unit looking at the two areas identified, namely: 3.1.1 and 3.1.6.

There were different interpretations placed by staff on the evidence they reviewed together with a variety of reasons offered by them for the basis upon which decisions were made.

Student 1 achieved 'competent' for 3.1.1 by half the staff and 'competent' for 3.1.6 on only one occasion. Those members of staff who awarded 'not yet competent' felt that there was a lack of detail in the evidence provided by this student.

Student 2 achieved 'competent' on five occasions for both competence statements but it is interesting to note that, on the two occasions when 'not yet competent' was awarded, this was by different staff members. The reason for failure for 3.1.1 was given as lack of documentary evidence and 3.1.6 was due to the absence of evidence for emergency situations, although the remaining five members of staff were satisfied by the evidence provided by this student.

Student 3 was felt by five members of staff to be 'competent' for 3.1.1 and this was reduced to four members of staff for 3.1.6. One member of staff awarded 'not yet competent' for both of the competence statements with the reason given for this as the necessity to carry out an in-depth discussion with this candidate, as the evidence was being submitted through APL. It would appear that this member of staff would insist upon a more rigorous approach for a student using an APL mechanism.

Evidence produced by student 4 for 3.1.1 was considered by five members of staff to be inadequate, mainly due to the format in which it appeared and the lack of detail included. Only one member of staff awarded 'competent' for 3.1.6, the remainder giving the same reasons as in 3.1.1 above. This was the most consistent outcome of all, with all but one of the staff giving similar reasons for 'not yet competent' being awarded to this candidate.

Four members of staff felt that the evidence produced by student 5 for both 3.1.1 and 3.1.6 indicated 'not yet competent' due to the lack of detail submitted in the evidence. A number of staff commented that the student had simply produced a copy of the criteria statements and, despite the inclusion of a signed statement from a supervisor on work placement, the evidence lacked personal ownership.

Student 6 was awarded 'competent' by four members of staff for 3.1.1, reducing to three for 3.1.6. The reason given for awarding 'not yet competent' was insufficient detail, or lack of detail, in the evidence submitted.

The general procedures adopted by staff at an accreditation session had displayed consistency in such areas as question and answer technique. They all stated that they would use this technique to establish validity and ownership of the evidence presented by the individual student. Discussion between the staff member and student invariably took place when clarification of achievement of the range statement and performance criteria was thought necessary to ensure that they had been met.

As can be seen from the analysis above, a variety of outcomes resulted when competent, qualified staff, who are experienced in accreditation, reviewed the same pieces of evidence and carried out assessment procedures. Despite the consistency of the general procedures adopted by staff, this was not reflected in the awards which they gave to the students in this micro-study. There was in the case of student 4 a strong feeling by five out of six staff that this student was not competent in either of the competence outcomes. Again student 2 was felt competent by five out of six staff in both competence outcomes. There still, however, remained one member of staff who did not subscribe to the consensus of opinion for both of these students in both competence statements. Other students' outcomes varied from two disagreements, to half the staff awarding differing assessment outcomes.

It would appear that the discrepancies often occur as to the level of acceptability of the evidence submitted by the student. The number of students who were awarded 'not yet competent' in this study would perhaps indicate an over-zealous approach being adopted by some members of staff with regard to sufficiency and appropriateness of evidence submitted.

The study has highlighted the issues involved in the assessment of NVQ competences. It would appear that differences do exist between the Lead Body's definition of 'competence' and the interpretations made by the assessors, who, as can be seen in this micro-study, differed considerably in some cases about the evidence presented to them by students. Inconsistency in the interpretation of sufficiency and acceptability of evidence would indicate the need for clearer guidance to be issued by Lead Bodies if confusion and diversity of interpretation are to be avoided.

Conclusions

One of the major problems identified by the study and emerging in discussions with staff involved with NVQ delivery is in the wording used by the Lead Bodies, which, it is felt, is prone to misinterpretation. As stated, staff following Lead Body Assessor Awards are struggling to interpret the terminology given within the guidelines for these awards and one of the positive features has been the development of a more sympathetic approach to their own students, who are carrying out the arduous task of interpretation of competence statements

Some concern was felt over the misinterpretation of assessment taking place in a criterion-referenced context, whereby comparisons were made by staff on occasion in a way which would be suitable in a norm-referenced assessment mechanism but which is totally unacceptable in an NVQ assessment mode. Inappropriate elements were also mentioned by staff during the assessment of evidence, which, although they could be classified as Reception activities, were not requirements included in the two competence statements under review.

A year after the study took place internal verification procedures were put in place. Such procedures aim to address quality control and to enable some consistency in assessment to take place. The Internal Verifier samples evidence, checks that a suitable range of types of evidence is being used for assessment, talks to a sample of students, checks a sample of records and gives feedback to assessors including action points together with a record of the outcomes of the verification process. A cautionary note must surely be sounded concerning the amount of time involved in this process, which would perhaps be seen as part of a lecturer's workload, and the amount of remission from teaching which this might or might not involve. In the present cost-conscious further education culture it is difficult to predict the amount of remission which would be considered reasonable.

The internal verification system appears to be working effectively but, as with many new systems, it is implemented and then little evaluation appears to be carried out to ascertain its value and appropriateness. Much would appear still to depend upon the emphasis and importance placed upon internal verification activities by the management teams in colleges.

In addition there are External Verifiers whose role is to ensure standardisation of assessment. As numbers of NVQ candidates increase within centres, the workloads of both Internal and External Verifiers are obviously increasing. Currently, in a day's visit, an External Verifier must incorporate verification of as many as four or five NVQ levels, including reviewing work, speaking to candidates, answering queries, carrying out reporting procedures and paper work.

An External Verifier carries out these activities on a part-time basis, often being employed as a full-time lecturer in another institution with a limited amount of time available to make visits to centres. Lead Bodies have stated that they prefer External Verifiers to be currently attached in a delivery capacity to centres, but are finding it increasingly difficult to attract staff to carry out this role. They are, therefore, obliged to employ retired staff who are able to devote the necessary time but who lack current experience (especially of the ever-changing NVQ criteria!).

Factors such as the need to retain students, and outcome-related funding, place additional burdens upon further education colleges battling between successful outcomes for students and the maintenance of sound quality assurance programmes. Many college staff feel threatened by outside providers, who are also very conscious of the need for their students to succeed in an outcome-related environment. Those training providers remaining have seen many of their fellow providers' establishments close and are anxious to ensure that their students will achieve NVQ awards in order that they may receive payment for them.

In the future, the kind of assessment techniques to which students are exposed, together with the greater self-esteem to be gained from a sense of achievement, and the increased motivation generated to undertake additional training, will increasingly play an important part in strengthening an organisation's position against its competitors. A qualification which has been earned through an honest endeavour to meet the necessary criteria, and the sense of personal fulfilment when it is achieved, will hopefully result in NVQs being implemented which are conducive to the growth of a competent workforce. Consistency in assessment is critical to this situation coming about.

References

Chown, A. and Last, J. (1993), *Concerning Competence*. NATFHE Journal, Spring 1993.

Gealy, N. (1993), *Development of NVQs and SVQs at Higher Levels*. Competence and Assessment, Issue 21, Employment Department's Strategy Unit, Sheffield: Employment Department, p4.

Hallmark, A.T. and Horton, D. (1991), *Personal Competence model: further refinement*. Sheffield: Employment Department.

Hyland, T. (1992), *Meta-competence, Metaphysics and Vocational Expertise*. Competence and Assessment, Issue 20, Employment Department's Strategy Unit, Sheffield: Employment Department, p20.

Jack, M., Goodman, H. and Newberry, G. (1993), *Assessment of Learning Outcomes - the BTEC Experience*. Competence and Assessment, Issue 21, Employment Department's Strategy Unit, Sheffield: Employment Department, p17.

Jessup, G. (1991), *Outcomes: NVQs and the emerging model of education and training*. London: Falmer Press.

Johnson, C. (1993), *Judging Evidence in NVQ Assessment*, unpublished, The University of Huddersfield.

Johnson, C.E. and Blinkhorn, S.F. (1992), *Validating NVQ Assessment*. Competence and Assessment, Issue 20, Employment Department's Strategy Unit, Sheffield: Employment Department, p10.

Maclure, S. (1991), *Missing Links: the Challenge to Further Education*. London: Policy Studies Institute.

Mitchell, L. and Cuthbert, T. (1989), *Insufficient evidence? The final report of the competency testing project*. Glasgow: SCOTVEC.

Mitchell, L. and Sturton, J. (1993). Competence and Assessment, Issue 21, Employment Department's Strategy Unit, Sheffield: Employment Department, p22.

Moran, D. (1991), *The role of knowledge in competence-based measurement, Education, N.115, pp8-9*. Competence and Assessment, Issue 20, Employment Department's Strategy Unit, Sheffield: Employment Department, p22.

National Council for Vocational Qualifications (1991), *Emerging Issues in the Utilisation of NVQs: Research and Development Report 5*. London: NCVQ.

National Council for Vocational Qualifications (1992), *National Standards for Assessment and Verification Report 13*. London: NCVQ.

Tuxworth, E. (1984) in Burke, J. *Competency-based Education and Training*. London: Falmer Press.

Wolf, A. (1988), *Assessing Knowledge and Understanding: methods and research priorities for a competence-based system*. Report to NCVQ, London: NCVQ.

Wolf, A. (1991), *Unwrapping Knowledge and Understanding from Standards of Competence*, Black and Wolf; op.cit. pp31-8.

3 TDLB units - threat or improvement?

David Neve

Abstract

The introduction of a competence-based curriculum has many implications for those engaged in the process of delivering vocational education and training. In particular the final responsibility for validating assessment procedures has shifted increasingly towards teachers, imposing on them a new form of accountability; which in turn has necessitated the compulsory meeting of Training and Development Lead Body (TDLB) standards by those engaged in assessing NVQ and GNVQ awards, where centres wish to achieve 'approved assessment centre status'. This process entails the certification of all staff whose roles include the assessment of competence within the NVQ/GNVQ framework. This paper examines the nature and significance of the kind of 'accountability' now required of teacher/assessors, in particular against a background of output-related funding, and discusses the appropriateness or otherwise of having to accredit staff with already existing competences. It is concluded that the undeniable benefits of the approach are barely commensurate with the drain upon college staff development resources which its implementation represents.

Introduction

Effective learning processes are typified by a number of key stages, for example the delivery of the material by the teacher, using a wide variety of possible strategies, followed by student activity aimed at the practice of routines or the internalising of concepts and/or principles (Child

1986). These in turn are often followed by assessment and by feedback gained during the assessment process. Thus the routine work of the teacher has traditionally involved assessment of learning and the provision of feedback to the teacher and student alike. Effective learning is unlikely to take place unless teachers are provided with information on which to base evaluation of their own performance and the learners in turn are provided with opportunities for evaluating their own progress (Curzon 1985). Assessment provides this valuable information and has therefore been a key feature of the effective teacher's work since Socrates and Plato taught at their local 'colleges'.

This situation is well understood within education and training circles and has been so for a great many years. Yet the assessment role of the teacher in vocational education and training has come under close scrutiny and undergone dramatic change with the introduction of the competence-based curriculum and the associated development of NVQs and GNVQs. In order that they may assess competence and satisfy the criteria of the National Council for Vocational Qualifications, experienced teachers have now to prove their competence to perform the assessment process before they can be classified as 'Approved Assessors' and carry out the assessments necessary for candidates seeking NVQ/GNVQ awards (Giles 1993). Many, if not all, awarding bodies require that their approved assessors undertake this process before January 1995 and obtain the Training and Development Lead Body Assessor Award standards (Carter 1993). (Originally the deadline was to be 1994 although an extension was granted late in 1993.)

These approved assessors will now be 'licensed' by the lead body or awarding body and allocated an assessor number, which must be entered on all assessment documentation. This represents an obvious shift in accountability since, prior to the introduction of competence-based NVQs, ultimate responsibility for the assessment procedures was borne by the awarding bodies through a system of external moderation. Whilst teachers often designed assessment programmes in some awards, in others these were designed and written by the awarding body. Teachers may have had responsibility for drawing up the marking scheme and model answers (although this was not universally the case, as some awarding bodies actually produced machine-marked tests (as in Brickwork - CGLI 5888 - 1972 to 1992) or supplied the model answers and marking scheme); but the one common feature of these systems was the fact that responsibility for the quality of the assessment process was firmly rooted with the awarding bodies, not with the teacher/assessor.

This system of the licensing of assessors changes this situation quite dramatically. As a result, the recording of assessor numbers on all assessment returns made to the awarding bodies provides a system which makes the assessor totally accountable for any assessment decisions. Where assessors are required to enter their numbers, a single candidate's assessment can be traced back to the individual assessor (CITB 1990/1991); thus self-regulation within the system becomes the accepted norm, whereas in the past the general oversight of the BTEC, RSA, or CGLI assessment process was the domain of the external moderator. At the same time, in another move to self-regulate and increase accountability, Funding Council policies require colleges to set up strategies for quality assurance (FEFC 1993); while the FEFC are also actively encouraging the use of performance indicators linked to achievement of NVQs and GNVQs to assess the quality of individual curriculum areas in colleges. In this climate of local and individual responsibility, moreover, the assessor and his/her first-line supervisor (internal verifier) are made doubly accountable, with their assessment decisions inevitably having a direct relationship with the level of funding which the college attracts through output-related funding mechanisms and the assessment of the college's quality by FEFC inspectors.

It is against this background of the pinpointing of responsibility for assessment decisions, of course, that the requirement of 're-qualification' arises, the point being that the licensing is made conditional on their achieving the TDLB units of competence (Carter 1993). The first-line assessor, furthermore, is not the only member of the assessor team to experience the need for this formal certification of competence to perform the assessment role which experienced teachers have engaged in since mass education and training policies became the norm. In further developments designed to make the institutions more accountable for their own actions, the first-line supervisor of the assessment team must also prove his/her competence to supervise the assessment process. Thus, the 'internal verifier' was born and, along with the title, another TDLB standard covering the competence expected in such a role - the TDLB unit D34 applies to this particular function. (Awarding bodies generally require each curriculum area to have at least one internal verifier to oversee the assessment programme and to ensure that the correct procedures are adopted. In fairness, though this may appear to be a new procedure, college staff have for some considerable time answered to first-line managers, often referred to as section heads and heads of department.)

All this would be understandable enough in a system starting from scratch. However, under traditional arrangements, the assessment process was finally coordinated by teams of external moderators appointed from within colleges (although this was not an exclusive arrangement, as some awarding bodies (BTEC for example) actively encouraged people from industry and commerce to take on the role of external moderator). In many cases, however, the external moderator appointed to specific curriculum areas was employed as teacher/manager in a college offering similar programmes to those of the college being moderated. Thus, a great many staff across the country had wide experience of moderating roles and underwent regular training in the process, in order to keep abreast of awarding body policies or new assessment strategies. Yet, despite the existence of armies of people with vast moderating experience, the onset of NVQs and GNVQs has created a perceived need to ensure that these people also have 'qualifications' in order that they might carry out their duties effectively. TDLB Unit D35 provides the external moderator with an opportunity to gain accreditation for the role of external verifier. One is left wondering what the difference between external *moderator* and external *verifier* roles might be. The fact remains that staff engaged in the external verification process have to prove their competence to perform the role to national standards.

Now of course competence can be awarded on the basis of accrediting the assessor or indeed the internal and external verifier with the competence she/he already owns. This allows the experienced assessor/verifier to use her/his existing knowledge, understanding and skill of the assessment process to gain the assessor/verifier award through accreditation of prior learning, achievement or experience. Clearly, in this situation, the existing competence is recognised and little or no further training is necessary, prior to gaining the award. However, if the TDLB standards recognise the existence of competence and the system takes account of competence gained in carrying out assessment on the job or through previous training and qualifications, one wonders why the awards are necessary in the first place. Yet when, in the construction curriculum area, attempts were made to have the existing competence accredited automatically, on the basis that it was gained through experience and in many cases certified at a much higher level through the award of Certificate in Education or even BEd or MEd, the initiative failed, as competence was not regarded as proven through the gaining of academic awards. Assessors had to prove they could *perform* assessment tasks within the stated criteria, and clearly the award of a Certificate in Education gained previously was not made on this basis. Whilst in most cases further training has not been necessary, the fact remains that great numbers of FE college staff have undergone 'training' in the development of portfolios of evidence of their competence to assess or verify - often to assist them in determining the meaning of some rather verbose elements of competence and performance criteria. Indeed, after two years in existence the TDLB National Standards are to be revised (Canning 1994) and hopefully presented in terms which can be fully understood by the users.

Some reflections

Whilst the assessor becomes accountable for the assessment decisions taken, improvement in the quality of the assessment and in standardisation across the nation is questionable, especially when covert pressure is applied to assessors by institutional managers working with funding models based upon the numbers of nationally approved qualifications achieved in the institution (The Observer, March 1994). There can be little doubt that a system of funding based on results makes the assessor accountable not only for the assessment of competence but also for a significant proportion of the funding units which each college can attract. Little concrete evidence exists on which to base this perception although some candidates, assessed by *some* private training providers, have been seriously wanting when seeking progression from NVQ Level II to Level III at their local college (a fact which has been discussed at length by Heads of Construction in many colleges). Candidates have needed to undertake considerable amounts of remedial work to repeat competences that they had apparently achieved elsewhere, thus raising considerable doubts about the quality of the assessment process in some areas.

Given that a great number of well-qualified teachers and managers with vast experience of the assessment process have now to undergo further accreditation to comply with the awarding body regulations, one could be forgiven for taking a somewhat cynical view of the fact that these awards have presented the awarding bodies with wonderful opportunities to raise huge sums of money from registration fees, log book sales and attendance at courses - money which incidentally has been found from staff development budgets which have been increasingly reduced over the last year or two. The imposition of training courses for teachers with experience of the assessment process must be questionable, especially when related to the fees charged for such activities. Some schemes in operation require the production of portfolios of 'dissertation' proportions, with the consequent over-inflation of the awards beyond their NVQ Level III status. If we must have these awards, let us at least keep them within their recognised level of achievement.

Having said that, as one who has undertaken the development of a portfolio of evidence and assessment of his own competence at assessing performance, this writer would be the first to recognise that there are some advantages for all staff engaged in the process of attaining the TDLB units. Firstly, the NVQ structure is fundamentally different to anything we have experienced in this country before. Clearly, some staff will have gained a great deal of awareness in relation to the whole business of assessing competence within the vocational qualification framework; yet too much emphasis has perhaps been placed in the past on awarding numerical or letter grades, even for practical work carried out by motor vehicle engineers, construction craft operatives or students working in the hotel and catering business. The development of assessment schemes based upon the criterion-referenced model is generally accepted, at least in the vocational training area.

Secondly, from the writer's experience gained through FEFC inspections, it is clear that the effectiveness and quality of feedback given to students is very variable. The TDLB units include national standards related to the method and quality of feedback given to students. The award accredits the assessor for this feedback role and again recognises the accountability of the teacher/assessor in the carrying out of this function. Initiatives which improve the overall quality of the FE system must be widely welcomed, provided that value for money can be achieved from the initial investment.

Thirdly, many teachers have been encouraged to work together within their curriculum teams, whilst building portfolios of evidence. Again through personal experience, gained whilst assessing 30 staff for the TDLB units at Brighton College, the writer has witnessed this process and discovered the benefits that team work inevitably brings to a curriculum area. The sharing of ideas and experiences can only assist the teacher in becoming more effective in all the roles expected today. To see the Assistant Principal working with main grade lecturers and actually taking advice from the lecturers was sobering indeed. Such sharing can only provide a more effective working relationship. The staff who undertook this group initiative to attain the TDLB Assessor Award also had the opportunity to evaluate, in a constructive manner, the assessment processes that existed at the particular institution and clearly identified, for themselves, the strengths and weaknesses of these processes. The evidence collected for portfolio development tended to ensure that some weaknesses within the college assessment systems were attended to almost immediately after they were recognised. The process of attaining the TDLB standards had led the candidates to review some current practices and to make changes where these were seen as necessary.

The process of collecting evidence of one's competence to perform the assessment function also assisted in determining whether one was using the appropriate procedures and practices. In itself the whole experience of undertaking the assessor award was effective staff development in its own right. There can be little argument that the teacher/assessor has become more accountable with the introduction of competence-based qualifications: the current opportunities to review current practice and evaluate processes can only enhance the well-being of the FE system as a whole.

However, the costs involved for this training and accreditation of teacher/assessors in competence, where in many cases they already own and use them in their day-to-day work, could be considered an over-zealous use of public resources. Is it really necessary to re-qualify staff who have undergone a broad range of staff development and initial training courses or programmes for their roles? The vast majority of staff working in FE do undergo initial teacher-training, with many progressing to graduate and postgraduate awards as their careers develop.

Supporters of the NVQ assessor qualification would argue that it is not necessary to undergo training or even re-training where the existence of competence can be proven. The fact is that this may well be the case. However, the cost of putting one member of staff through an APL/APLA process is often as costly as starting anew with training programmes, let alone putting the vast majority of the staff in a college with, say, 200 academics through re-training and assessment programmes aimed at skills they already possess. In a situation of increasing accountability for the funds allocated to the FE colleges, one could be forgiven for questioning the wisdom of the whole TDLB initiative, in terms of the financial burden this has created. Most college managers would welcome the chance to allocate the resources used for TDLB qualification and training for more pressing areas of development. There is little hard evidence to indicate that teachers employed in the FE sector are or have been deficient in their assessment of learners and in turn need substantial retraining or qualification. Indeed, many deficiencies associated with assessment practice can be attributed to the assessment strategies themselves, for example the social weaknesses associated with grading learners under a norm-referenced assessment procedure, or the emphasis on over-simplified task-based assessment under the NVQ assessment model.

In the final analysis, the huge cost of accrediting teacher/assessor competence to carry out what is after all one very small element of the vast array of roles that present teaching staff carry out (Cook 1992) may be seen as short-sighted.

On the other hand it can be argued that staff who undertake the building of portfolios of evidence in relation to national standards of competence will be well prepared for the whole business of guiding their own learners through this process, together with the associated interpretation of performance criteria and range statements - everyday terms in the NVQ/GNVQ framework. The question remains perhaps:

was this really the best and most cost-effective way to achieve this particular objective?

References

Carter, J. (1993), *Assessing Quality in NVQs*. The NVQ Monitor, March 1993. London: NCVQ.

CGLI (1972), *Brickwork and Masonry*, Syllabus 588. London: City and Guilds.

Child, D. (1986), *Psychology and the Teacher* (4th ed.), London: Cassell.

Cook, M.J. (1992), *The Role of the Teacher: an investigation of the work of teachers working with post-16 year old students or trainees*, Polytechnic of Huddersfield.

CITB (1991), *National Vocational Qualifications - Approved Assessor's Handbook*, Bircham Newton: CITB.

Curzon, L.B. (1985), *Teaching in Further Education*, (3rd ed.), London: Cassell.

FEFC (1993), *Assessing Achievement - circular 43/93*, Coventry: FEFC.

Giles, C. (1993), *Assessors and Verifiers - a Question of Quality*. The NVQ Monitor, Autumn. London: NCVQ.

Hugell, B. (1994), *Colleges in Scandal of Exam Passes*. The Observer, 27:3:94.

TDLB, (1993), *News Brief*. Winter Newsletter, Rugby: Training and Development Lead Body.

4 Aspects of competence in a nursing context

John Sheehan

Abstract

In this paper the issue of competence is discussed in relation to the pre-registration and post-registration levels of nursing, and more briefly in relation to Health Care Assistants. Rule 18 competencies and Benner's (1984) model of skill acquisition are considered and so are the proposals for the post-registration education of nurses. Examples of current research are cited. In the conclusion, points are raised concerning the adequacy of the competence approach in a nursing context.

Introduction

The concept of competence is taken as a given as far as this paper is concerned since the matter is dealt with elsewhere within these papers, and it is not proposed to repeat or rehearse the arguments for and against the various characteristics of the concept which appear in the rapidly growing literature. It is necessary, however, to deal briefly with the nursing context in which the notion of competence is being considered. Nursing may be considered to be an umbrella term for a service which is provided for a whole range of people including children, adults, elderly people, those with mental health problems and those with learning difficulties. It takes place in a variety of settings such as hospitals, where specialities abound such as ear, nose and throat, gynaecological, intensive care and medical nursing. To these may be added ophthalmology, orthopaedics, surgical and renal nursing. This list, though long, is meant to be representative rather than a comprehensive list of nursing specialities. Whilst much nursing takes place in hospitals, it also takes place increasingly in people's homes as a consequence of a greater emphasis on community care. Nursing also takes place in the workplace where occupational health nurses look after the health of the workers.

This brief characterisation of the nature of nursing reflects something of the diverse nature of the activity. However, while not losing sight of its diversity, this paper will focus on the issue of competence in relation to two levels of nursing function: first, the pre-registration level, which takes account of student nurses in training; second, the post-registration level which takes account of qualified nurses taking part in programmes of professional development. It is also intended to mention briefly the issue of Health Care Assistants because they work closely with nurses, and their training is competence-based.

Pre-registration

Nursing takes place within a statutory framework. The United Kingdom Central Council (UKCC) for Nursing, Midwifery and Health Visiting regulates nursing, midwifery and health visiting professions in the public interest, and it is clearly in the public interest to have nurses who are competent to do their job. The UKCC was established by the Nurses, Midwives and Health Visitors Act 1979. Section 2 (1) of that Act states that 'the principal functions of the Central Council shall be to establish and improve standards of training and professional conduct'. Thus, the UKCC is first and foremost concerned about the interests of the public, but in meeting that responsibility it is also concerned with standards of training. The baseline which is frequently cited is safety in practice. Practitioners in any aspect of nursing are expected to carry out their practices and procedures in a safe manner. However, many nurses would seek to advance beyond the baseline and would strive for excellence in practice.

While the Nurses, Midwives and Health Visitors Act 1970 provides the legislative framework, many detailed aspects are set out in Statutory Instruments. In the case of competencies, those are set out in Statutory Instrument No.1456, the Nurses and Midwives Act 1979, Clause 18A. The competencies set out in Statutory Instrument No.1456 are those which relate to student nurses on Project 2000 courses (UKCC 1985). In order to be awarded a licence to practise, that is, to become a Registered Nurse, student nurses are required to achieve Rule 18A competencies.

Thirteen competencies are linked within Rule 18A. The intention here is not to list all 13 of them but to give a flavour of what they encompass. Before the introduction of Project 2000 courses the study of nursing was based on illness and ill-health. Apart from raising the academic level of study from Certificate to Diploma level, the introduction of Project 2000 shifted the focus of nursing studies to some extent from ill-health to health, though ill-health obviously remains an important issue. There are, thus, Project 2000 competencies concerned with health and health promotion as well as with ill-health. In Project 2000 courses, there is an emphasis on the use of research to inform practice and this is one of the competencies. Legal and ethical issues have implications for all, but in nursing where a patient's intellectual functions may be impaired because of injury or disease processes, these issues assume a particular significance. As might be expected, there are in Project 2000 courses competencies on both the legal and ethical aspects of nursing. Communication skills may be regarded as a pre-requisite in any activity which involves working with people, such as nursing, and there is a competence concerned with that issue.

In current debates, there is a good deal of emphasis placed on adopting a holistic approach to nursing. Without mentioning it, specifically, this notion seems to be implicit in Rule 18 (j). This competence is concerned with the identification of the physical, psychological, social and spiritual needs of the patient or client. This competence also includes an awareness of the values and concepts of individual care. It includes the ability to devise a plan of care, and to contribute to its implementation and evaluation; and the demonstration of the application of the principles of a problem-solving approach to the practice of nursing.

Rule 18 (j) competence as outlined above presents two problems. First, it involves so many variables that it is likely to be difficult to discriminate between them when it comes to assessment. Moreover, the elements which are included in the competence are on a wide range of human abilities, which means that a wide range of evidence would be needed in order to determine whether a nurse was competent or not. Even if there is a way of assessing the many and diverse variables within Rule 18 (j), there is a potential danger that the resulting assessment may be at a rather superficial level, because of the complexity of the competence and the fact that there is rarely unlimited time available for the assessment process.

The reform of nurse education which resulted in the introduction of Project 2000 courses has meant radical changes in how nursing, in its many aspects, is approached. One of these is a change from the previous task-centred to an individualised approach to the delivery of nursing care. There was dissatisfaction with the task-centred approach and Menzies (1970), for example, wrote about a kind of depersonalisation or an elimination of individual distinctiveness in both nurse and patient. She went on to say that nurses often talk about patients, not by name, but by bed number or by their disease or diseased organ. When Rule 18 (j) competencies are viewed against that background, it is perhaps possible to understand how they came about. There was pressure within nursing, and, indeed, a good deal of consensus concerning the matter, to adopt an approach which was individualised rather than task-centred, holistic rather than atomistic and so on. There are many reasons for welcoming the changes. However, the assessment of these competencies ought to be a matter for continuing concern to ensure that the public is indeed served by competent nurses.

Other Rule 18 (j) competencies include working in a team, recognising the limits of individual competence and referral of problems to the appropriate agency/agencies. Finally, there is a competence concerned with the assignment of duties and the supervision, teaching and monitoring of the process.

. In the process of achieving competence in the practice of nursing, it has been identified that nurses, like other professional groups, progress through several developmental stages. Benner (1984), a much cited source in nursing literature, has identified five distinct phases in the process of achieving competency. The five phases are: novice, advanced beginner, competent, proficient and expert. Benner's work has been very influential in nurse education and, therefore, needs to be considered further, particularly as she has set out criteria for assessing performances in practice.

The criteria that apply at the novice phase of Benner's continuum are that the student is able to follow rules, policies and procedures in the particular setting, but requires constant supervision.

Knowledge of the rules, policies and procedures which apply is also required at the advanced beginner phase; but some progress is expected since there is an expectation of flexibility in the interpretation of these rules. The implication is that the need for supervision diminishes somewhat.

At the competent phase of Benner's continuum, the student is expected to discriminate between and to choose which rules, policies, procedures and so on apply in particular circumstances. The student is also expected to anticipate outcomes and to provide rationales for the interpretations reached and the intervention made. At the novice phase, the assumption is that the student lacks economy of effort in practice; but at the competent phase economy of effort is expected as an indication of progress on Benner's continuum.

To be proficient means that the student is able to take a holistic view of issues and problems and can determine priorities. The student is expected to demonstrate an intuitive feel for situations and solutions. (The intuitive feel is likely to present problems when it comes to assessment.) The student is also expected to demonstrate a skilled performance.

In the fifth and final phase, which is the expert phase in Benner's continuum, the student is expected to be able to work with a holistic view and an intuitive grasp of the issues and problems. At this phase, the student is also expected to make informed choices; predict outcomes; demonstrate economy of effort; step out of rule-following, adapt rules and maintain safe practices. Finally, the student at the expert phase is expected to identify new areas for investigation, development and change.

There are at least two points worthy of discussion arising from Benner's (1994) model of competence acquisition. The first concerns the language used. At face value, it would seem that there is a clear-cut distinction between novice at one end and expert at the other end of the continuum. It is when one looks more closely that this initial clarity becomes less clear. In Fergusson (1986) we find that the term novice is synonymous with beginner. The second phase in Benner's continuum is advanced beginner; but we find that beginner is synonymous with novice. Competent is the next phase in Benner's continuum and we find that competent is synonymous with proficient, which is the fourth phase of the continuum. Moreover, we find that expert, which is the fifth and final stage, is synonymous with proficient. If, as seems to be the case, the descriptors used for the different phases of Benner's continuum can be used interchangeably, there must be a question as to how they will discriminate when it comes to assessing competence. It might be argued that the criteria set out for each of the phases make it possible for meaningful discriminations to be assessed. If this line of argument is accepted, some concern must remain concerning the robustness of the key descriptors in Benner's continuum. It might be argued that to indulge in the semantics surrounding the issue is to be unduly pedantic. However, important decisions are made which are based on the use of these descriptors. Since such decisions have important implications for the students concerned and for patient care, in order to ensure equity in the assessment process constant vigilance is needed: there is no room for complacency.

The second point about Benner's model which ought to be commented on concerns the nature of learning, though this would be applicable to any model based on a continuum. Learning rarely takes place in neat incremental steps. Sometimes the learning curve may be very steep; at other times there may be plateaux when the learning process slows down while what has been learned is consolidated. Then there are individual differences concerning the rate of skill acquisition so that the amount of practice needed varies. The point is, if Benner's continuum is to be used, given its weaknesses at the level of language as set out above, it ought to be used in a sensitive manner which takes account of individual differences concerning the nature of learning and the need for practice.

Current research by McAndrew (in preparation) adds a new dimension to the assessment of competence in a nursing context. The research is based on Benner's (1984) model, which McAndrew accepts since it is so widely used in nursing. The new dimension which McAndrew's study is concerned with is that of self-assessment of clinical nursing competence, and he makes the point that, up to now, nurses have not been helped to assess their own competence. He draws on the work of Rowntree (1977) and Rogers (1983) to support the notion of self-assessment by students. Whilst a good deal of work on the study remains to be done, the indications are that it will be possible, as intended, to develop a conceptual model of the process of the self-assessment of competence.

Post-registration

Nursing education, as already suggested, has changed radically in recent years. In the case of student nurses on pre-registration courses, the change has been to the Project 2000 approach to the nursing curriculum. Some of the issues relating to competence have been discussed above. Continuing education is a matter for concern for any profession, because of the need to keep up to date with developments and practices. The current policy for the continuing education of qualified nurses has been set out and has been reported as the Post-Registration and Education Practice Project, which has been abbreviated to PREPP (UKCC 1990). A related document sets out the Code of Professional Practice (UKCC 1992). While the principal purpose of the UKCC is to serve and protect the public and to influence policy and practice for the benefit of patients and clients, it is the function of the National Boards of the constituent countries of the United Kingdom to implement these policies. This they do by validating and monitoring courses run by educational institutions, rather than delivering courses themselves.

In the case of England, the English National Board for Nursing, Midwifery and Health Visiting (ENB) has set out its framework for Continuing Professional Education for Nurses, Midwives and Health Visitors (ENB 1991). There are similarities between the UKCC's PREP (the final P has now been dropped since it is no longer a project) and the

ENB's Framework. These similarities include the use of a Credit Accumulation and Transfer Scheme (CATS), the need to prevent repetitious learning through the use of APL and APEL and degree level outcomes. But perhaps the similarity most relevant to this paper is the issue of competence. The PREPP proposal (UKCC 1990) was explicit about competencies at different levels such as primary specialist and advanced practice. The ENB (1994), among other publications about the matter, set out its 10 characteristics which are work-based and outcome-focused. The elements which make up the 10 characteristics are set out below.

Table 1: The ENB's 10 Characteristics

1.	Accountability	6.	Health Promotion
2.	Clinical Skills	7.	Staff Development
3.	Use of Research	8.	Resource Management
4.	Team Work	9.	Quality of Care
5.	Innovation	10.	Management of Change

There are some similarities between Rule 18A competencies, already mentioned, and the ENB's 10 characteristics, and perhaps it is not surprising that there should be continuity between pre-registration and post-registration competencies since it may be expected that those at pre-registration level would form a basis for development. The similarities concern competencies such as clinical skills; the use of research; team work and health promotion. Aspects which are not explicitly shared between Rule 18A competencies and the ENB's 10 characteristics include accountability; innovation; staff development; resource management; quality and the management of change. A student nurse, of course, is accountable, but overall accountability must rest with those in charge, since it would be unfair to hold an unqualified person ultimately accountable. Similarly, staff development, quality assurance and the management of change are issues which are beyond the remit of student nurses.

At the post-registration level of education discourse, there are opportunities for development on two planes. To take Benner's (1984) as an example, there are potential opportunities to develop towards the expert end of the continuum. The aspects in the 10 characteristics not found in Rule 18A provide the opportunity to develop new competencies and thus expand the professional horizons. The issue of competency-based education has received a fair amount of attention in the nursing literature, for example, Vaughan (1991), Ellie (1988) and Whittington and Boore (1988). McCloskey (1981) poses the view that it is the responsibility of the nurse education system to assist students to achieve the competencies for effective practice. It is suggested that in order to achieve this courses must be designed on a competency basis.

Current research by Delbridge (in preparation) makes use of Benner's continuum, that is, novice, advanced beginner, competent, proficient and expert for the assessment of competence in Accident and Emergency Nursing. The assessment tool developed also includes Benner's seven domains as follows: helping role; teaching-coaching; diagnosis; managing; therapeutic intervention; organisational and quality. It also includes a record of learning experiences and there are spaces for comments by students and mentors. This is a small-scale study involving eight students. The results so far indicate that this assessment tool does show promise, but more data would be needed before making a stronger claim for it.

Health care assistants

The introduction of Project 2000 courses means radical changes for nursing education and some of these have been mentioned in this paper. A change not yet mentioned concerns the position of the students within the nursing workforce. Previously, student nurses were an integral part of the workforce and there were complaints that they were often used as 'pairs of hands' and that their educational needs sometimes took second place to the demands of the service. Within the Project 2000 system this state of affairs has been reversed and the students' educational needs are paramount. Such a change had obvious staffing implications. To meet these, a new grade of staff, initially known as support workers and now mostly known as health care assistants, was introduced.

There was joy in nursing circles concerning the introduction of Project 2000, but the introduction of support workers was not universally welcomed and many questions were raised at the time, such as 'could the support worker training provide a short cut into nursing itself?' (Fardell 1989). There were fears that, following a period of support worker training, there could be a reduction in the time taken for nurse training and this would, to some extent, negate the perceived gains of Project 2000 courses. Rowden (1989) posed the question 'helper or hindrance' in relation to support workers. His view was that nurses and support workers would need to learn to co-exist, but a basis of this co-existence ought to be a clear definition of each other's roles. 'Support - not supplant' was the title of a paper by Holder (1989) and has a protectionist ring about it. He argued that the introduction of support workers could have advantages for nursing, but he makes the point that the training and expectations of support workers must be kept within strict bounds. Holder (1989) goes on to make the point that the entry gate to nursing must be carefully guarded and that *National Council for Vocational Qualifications* approved qualifications (NVQs) should not be acceptable for entry into nursing.

The introduction of Project 2000 courses needed the approval of the Department of Health (DOH), which has overall responsibility for the Health Service including making sure that it is adequately staffed by appropriately qualified people. In giving approval for the introduction of Project 2000 the DOH did so on the condition that support workers would be added to the workforce to ensure adequate staffing of the service. Johnston (1989) put it thus: 'like it or not, the support worker is integral to the Project 2000 deal; it is a straightforward quid pro quo'. The reaction of health care workers, which was largely a reaction to change, is no longer as strong as it was. There are now significant numbers of people on NCVQ courses at levels I-III and they are slowly becoming an integral part of the workforce of the Health Service.

Conclusion

Nursing has changed considerably (as already mentioned) in recent times. The Report of the Committee on Nursing (1972) under the Chairmanship of Professor Asa Briggs (now Lord Briggs) has had a major impact on nursing and has, among other things, resulted in the legislation which set up the new statutory body for nursing, the UKCC, already mentioned. The national boards, such as the ENB, similarly followed from this legislation.

A brief quotation from the Briggs Report is relevant to the issue of competence and it reads

> Within a changing social and medical context, nursing and midwifery, we believe, will continue to stand out as the major caring profession, certainly the one most in the mind of the public. The caring professions, as a whole, need to show kindness as well as intelligence and sympathy as well as skill....

Caring is not defined in the report, but has been defined elsewhere. According to Leininger (1988), caring is the central and unifying domain for the body of knowledge and practices in nursing.

These two sources, and others would support the view, suggest that the concept of caring is central to the activity of nursing and this poses problems for assessment of competence in a nursing context. To refer to the elements in the Briggs report, intelligence can be measured though there is a great deal of controversy surrounding the issue, but kindness perhaps presents a greater challenge. Similarly, the performance of manual skills can be assessed, but sympathy also presents a challenge. Leininger (1988) suggests that caring is the central and unifying domain for nursing knowledge and practices. It seems difficult to encompass this notion within a competency model. While much valuable work has been done and is being done, it appears that much remains to be done. If caring is accepted as being central to the activity of nursing, then there must be a question mark concerning the adequacy of the competence approach, as presently construed, to assessment in a context of nursing.

References

Benner, P. (1984), *From Novice to Expert: Excellence and Power in Clinical Nursing Practice*. London: Addison-Wesley.

Delbridge, D. (in preparation), Competence: a study of skill acquisition based on the novice to expert performance of registered nurses undertaking a course in accident and emergency nursing. MEd in progress, School of Education, The University of Huddersfield.

Ellis, R. (1988) (ed.), *Professional Competence and Quality Assurance in the Caring Profession*. London: Chapman and Hall.

English National Board for Nursing, Midwifery and Health Visiting (1991), *Framework for Continuing Professional Education for Nurses, Midwives and Health Visitors: Guide to Implementation*. London: ENB.

English National Board for Nursing, Midwifery and Health Visiting (1994), *Reframing the Framework: Guidelines for Managers*. London: ENB.

Fardell, J. (1989), Short Cut or Short Change? *Nursing Times* 85, 30-31.

Fergusson, R. (1986), *The New Nuttall Dictionary of English Synonyms and Antonyms*. London: Guild Publishing.

Holder, S. (1989), Support Workers: Support - not Supplant. *Nursing Times* 85, 83.

Johnston, C. (1989), Who is the Support Worker? *Nursing Times* 15, 26-27.

Leininger, M. (1988) (ed.), *Caring: an Essential Human Need*. Detroit: Wayne State University Press.

McAndrew, P.S. (in preparation), The Self-Assessment of Clinical

Nursing Competence. PhD in progress, School of Education, The University of Huddersfield.

McCloskey, J.C. (1981), The Effects of Nursing Education on Job Effectiveness: an overview of the literature. *Research in Nursing and Health* 4, 355-373.

Menzies, I.E.P. (1970), *The Functioning of Social Systems as Defence Against Anxiety*. London: Tavistock.

Report of the Committee on Nursing (1972) (*The Briggs Report*). London: HMSO.

Rogers, C.R. (1983), *Freedom to Learn for the 80's*. London: Merrill.

Rowden, R. (1989), Support Workers: help or hindrance? *Nursing Times* 85, 52.

Rowntree, D. (1977), *Assessing Students - How will we know them?* London: Harper and Row.

Statutory Instrument (1989), Nurses, Midwives and Health Visitors Approval Order, 1989. London: HMSO (S.I. No.1456).

United Kingdom Central Council for Nursing, Midwifery and Health Visiting (1986), *Project 2000: a New Preparation for Practice*. London: UKCC.

United Kingdom Central Council for Nursing, Midwifery and Health Visiting (1990), *Post-Registration and Education Practice Project for Nurses, Midwives and Health Visitors*. London: UKCC.

United Kingdom Central Council for Nursing, Midwifery and Health Visiting (1992), *Code for Professional Conduct for Nurses, Midwives and Health Visitors*. London: UKCC.

Vaughan, B. (1991) 'Providing Clinical Care' in *Becoming a Staff Nurse* (Lathlean, J. and Corner, S. eds.). London: Prentice Hall.

Whittington, D. and Boore, J. (1988) 'Competence in Nursing' in *Professional Competence and Quality Assurance in the Caring Professions* (Ellis, R. ed.). London: Chapman and Hall.

5 After the Smithers Report: claim and counter-claim

Peter McKenzie and Paul Oliver

Abstract

Recent months have seen continuing controversy over the NCVQ system of vocational qualifications, and the 'Smithers Report' (1993) has focused on a purported tendency of NVQs to be outcome-driven at the expense of underpinning knowledge and understanding. This paper seeks to provide an analysis of such claims, and of subsequent counter-claims by NCVQ. Besides the issue of the relationship between outcomes and knowledge, the paper also discusses the work context of the new qualifications, and aspects of the assessment of NVQs, including the general issue of quality control. It continues with some consideration of the way in which the debate (in particular as regards GNVQs) has partially turned on the question of student-centred learning; and concludes that simplifications and rhetoric on both sides have done less than justice to this important concept and to the valuable practices it encompasses.

Introduction

The development of the system of National Vocational Qualifications, with its associated use of a competence approach, has already had an enormous impact upon the world of education and training. It is rare that a major innovation is implemented without some degree of contention, and the introduction of NVQs is no exception. The competence or outcome-based model contains within it a number of very interesting conceptual issues, which are both of specific relevance to the NVQ system, yet also of importance on a wider scale. An example would be the status of 'theoretical' knowledge within what is essentially a skill-

49

based programme. A fundamental question arises here concerning the amount and nature of the knowledge which is reasonably required to support the notion of work-based competence in a particular area - a question that has recently been made pivotal in the debate arising from the so-called Smithers Report and the associated television programme. The purpose of this paper is to provide an analysis of this and other underlying issues; in the first place by a close consideration of some NCVQ material; thus remedying, it is hoped, the NCVQ's complaint (NCVQ 1994, p2) that 'at no stage in the television programme were any NVQs or GNVQs actually presented or anatomised in such a way that viewers or readers could judge their contents for themselves'; and, in the second place, by examining the documentation provided by NCVQ in response to the Report, which purports to demonstrate conclusively that the procedures and arrangements in place ensure that there will not be a knowledge deficit as a result of the implementation of NVQs. The analysis will, it is hoped, provide a 'critical' account rather than a 'criticism' of the NVQ system; nonetheless, it will be argued that such evidence is still, on the face of it, equivocal, and such as might leave any doubting Thomas uncomfortably in need of final reassurance.

Additionally to all this, and constituting a separate but related issue, some attention will be given to the quaint and even incantatory usage made, by both parties to the debate, of such terms as 'student-centred' (on the part of Smithers, 1993, p9, Box A), and 'prescriptive methods' (NCVQ 1994, p2). Here above all the protagonists seem to be talking past one another, each using an unclarified stipulative definition that can only confuse the reader by attaching negative connotations to each term, when what is really required is some serious consideration of what should, and should not, be student-centred in a curriculum; and of what should, and should not, be prescriptive.

Let us turn our attention now to concrete instances. One of the central features of National Vocational qualifications is the 'Element of Competence'. This is an expression of a specific area of work activity, stated in such a way that it describes, accurately and unambiguously, the things an individual should be capable of doing in that context. An element of competence should relate to the actual situation of the workplace and not a simulated context such as a training course (Employment Department 1991). It should describe an aspect of work-related behaviour which is capable of demonstration and, hence, assessment. Such behaviour is often termed an 'outcome'. An imaginary example of an element of competence could be:

> The candidate should be able to implement a stock control system in a large retail outlet.

An element contains typically a verb ('implement'); an object ('a stock control system') and the circumstances or context of the activity ('in a large retail outlet').

The element of competence circumscribes the general nature of the vocational activity in question, but does not state precisely how well the competence must be demonstrated. In other words, as it stands, the element of competence would be difficult to assess. If two different candidates were to implement a stock control system they would probably do it in different ways, placing emphasis on separate parts of the process. It would, however, be difficult to compare performance or competence in this type of situation.

The problem is resolved by writing 'performance criteria' for each element of competence. In the above example, performance criteria would state unambiguously the ways in which the stock control system would have to be implemented in order to count as an example of competence. Perhaps the key aspect of performance criteria is that they should enable the assessment of a candidate to be carried out, by matching performance in work-related situations against the criteria.

In addition to the performance criteria, 'range statements' are also written for each element of competence. Range statements describe the contexts in which elements of competence and performance criteria apply. Range statements are important, particularly where there are unanticipated or unusual vocational contexts.

In analysing this framework it will probably be easier to refer to a specific example of an element of competence, such as that quoted in Appendix B of the Guide to National Vocational Qualifications. This particular competence relates to candidates who are providing support to client groups such as the mentally handicapped or elderly, in order to help them look after themselves in a community or residential setting. This particular element is at NVQ Level II in Health Care (Enablement Care). The overall unit title is to 'Support the client in the management of domestic and/or personal resources'. The specific element of competence which we can discuss is to 'Support the client in maintaining a supply of personal clothing and linen'.

The first performance criterion relates to the safe disposal of 'soiled or infected linen and clothing' and to the need for the candidates to protect themselves from infection. This is clearly a very important aspect of health care, in the sense that it concerns the maintenance of a safe and healthy environment for both the client and the supporting worker or carer. However, if dirty linen and clothing are to be dealt with appropriately, then it is clearly important that the candidate can distinguish between clothing which is merely grimy because of everyday wear, and clothing which may be contaminated or infected. To be able to make this distinction surely demands an understanding (albeit perhaps of a basic nature) of the sources of bacterial infection, some different types of bacteria, optimal conditions for bacterial growth, and measures to be taken to reduce the risks of bacterial infection.

The way in which this performance criterion is worded gives the impression that the candidates would be required to show the appropriate disposal of soiled linen, and that measures (unspecified) had been taken to maintain their own hygiene. The point to be suggested here though is that it is surely insufficient for a candidate who claims competence to do this on one or two occasions. Would we not wish to reassure ourselves that the candidate understood the reasons for his or her actions?

There seems to be a danger here that a candidate could have placed soiled linen in a suitable location on just one or two occasions, and thus be assessed as competent. This competence may however be very superficial. If the candidate is not fully aware of the underlying reasons for action, then the action adopted in a range of varied future situations may not always be appropriate.

It is therefore argued that, in the case of this performance criterion, 'competent performance' is not sufficient. It should be supported by a clearly specified knowledge base which provides the understanding for the candidate to meet satisfactorily the requirements of new or unusual circumstances which may arise.

Another performance criterion illustrates a similar issue. In this criterion, the candidate is asked to ensure that the laundry area is clean and that equipment in the laundry is in 'safe working order'. This seems to beg the question as to how the candidate will know that electrical equipment is safe, without a certain limited grounding in domestic electricity. Presumably, for example, it will be essential for the candidate to recognise when a plug is incorrectly wired. Again, it is the question of underlying knowledge. It is difficult to imagine how a candidate can be certain that laundry equipment is safe to use, without specific tuition in those aspects of safety and equipment maintenance which are relevant to the context. One would feel much more confident if there was a list of those aspects of equipment safety in which all candidates would receive training.

The issue of underlying knowledge is not unconnected with the range statements for a particular group of performance criteria. In the case of this particular unit, the client groups which are envisaged are those with learning difficulties, mental illness, physical handicap, and also elderly people. The important point here is that these client groups do not represent a homogeneous group. Clients with physical handicap may clearly have very high levels of intelligence and understanding, yet may suffer from limited manual dexterity. They may, for example, have difficulty actually using washing machines. On the other hand, clients with learning difficulties may, in principle, have little difficulty manipulating machinery, but have problems relating to understanding.

The very different needs of these two client groups thus require a distinct approach on the part of the candidate. One person may have a sophisticated understanding of bacterial infection and the ways in which soiled linen should be treated. Another person may have difficulty in understanding when clothing is unsafely dirty. One could argue that a truly competent candidate should be fully aware of the extent to which different client groups are capable of absorbing information and understanding.

In terms of knowledge, then, the argument is that the candidate should have a basic understanding of the concepts which underlie the performance criteria. These concepts should be specified, so that it is clear that certain knowledge elements relate to particular performance criteria. In addition, these knowledge elements should relate to the range statements and to the different contexts in which vocational competence will be assessed.

In all fairness to the NVQ model it should be added that it is conceded in this unit, that knowledge evidence 'may be necessary'. However, this rather vague statement gives no specific guidance about knowledge elements which, it is argued, are necessary for true vocational competence.

Again, trainers in some parts of the country may incorporate some elements of knowledge, while in other areas, different aspects of knowledge may be emphasised. This would clearly lead to differential standards. Both these issues are discussed further below, but on the face of it some kind of precise specification as advocated above would seem desirable.

Another central concept of the NVQ system is that competence should not be assessed in terms of the length of time that an individual has been training. Competence is not conceived as an ability which takes a certain length of course to acquire. It is acknowledged that different individuals acquire competence in different ways, and that people learn skills by different strategies. The NVQ system involves the assessment of candidates when they have the potential to demonstrate competence, not when they have spent a specified amount of time in training or at work.

Similarly, competence is not regarded as a function of any particular style or mode of training. Different individuals may acquire skills from a variety of work-based experiences and training courses. Some individuals may learn better in one context than another. It is also envisaged that age should not affect whether an individual can be assessed. In some occupations, there may be legal restrictions concerning age, but apart from these, it is not conceived that age should be a factor in excluding an individual from the possibility of assessment.

Now this approach certainly seems to have much to commend it, particularly in terms of equality of opportunity. There are no extraneous conditions which seem to apply: when an individual demonstrates the potential to achieve competence, then he or she can be assessed. The notion of open access to assessment seems to have many significant advantages, particularly for mature students. Many adults may have acquired skills in a variety of contexts, and NCVQ requires that arrangements be made available by awarding bodies for individuals to be accredited for their prior learning.

One possible drawback to an assessment process which takes no account of the length of time spent in training, however, is that vocational competence may be seen as a series of fragmented skills. One of the main functions of a training course of specific length is to socialise individuals into the norms and values of a particular profession. Trainees are exposed to the influence of practised professionals who can serve as effective role models. There is an opportunity for trainees to reflect on the standards and values of the profession, over a sustained period of time. Similarly, trainers can exercise professional influence over new entrants, and help to achieve continuity of standards and approaches.

The central advantage of the course of training was that it enabled new entrants to acquire a sense of the total profession. The danger of the incremental approach within open access assessment is that training in vocational competence is seen as a series of separate skills. The trainee may not ultimately link these together in a total vision of a profession. The argument therefore is that the whole is greater than the sum of the parts.

The incremental approach to training represents what might be termed a 'functionalist' analysis of the workplace. In other words, one identifies the discrete elements of a job, and assembles a training programme to meet this particular needs analysis. However, such a process may be ultimately reductivist. That is, the very act of breaking down workplace functions into separate units results in the loss of some overarching and important aspect of the work role. Michael Polanyi (1958) has referred to this type of understanding as 'tacit knowledge'. Although NVQs are clearly predicated upon the concept of the analysis of training functions into separate components, one might equally well focus upon the synthesis of separate skills into an overall role. This awareness of the total work-related role represents a different focus for training, and one which stresses the generic knowledge and skills which accompany the total job context.

The recent report on NCVQ by Professor Alan Smithers (1993) has focused sharply on the relationship between competence and knowledge, raising the sorts of questions that have been examined above. As mentioned already however, in an attempt at reassurance, and believing that the evidence will speak for itself, NCVQ (1994) in a response to the Smithers Report has sought to demonstrate that there are indeed important knowledge components incorporated within their vocational qualifications. They attach sample Units from a variety of occupations, each of these broken down into Elements, and thence into Performance Evidence and Criteria, and Knowledge Evidence (for supplementing performance evidence) and Criteria. Although it is made clear that Performance Evidence is to be regarded as the primary basis for judgments, supplementary evidence, represented by knowledge exhibited in written tests and oral response, is also acknowledged as significant. On the face of it they may seem to rebut the charges of laying inadequate stress on knowledge in NVQs; and it is this claim that requires some further attention here, if we are to form some sense of the justice, or otherwise, of Smithers' critique.

Certainly, in the examples offered in the Response, a good deal of knowledge is itemised. Consider, for example, the Evidence Specification for the proposed Level III qualification 'Configure, Commission and Coordinate Electrical Installation' (NCVQ 1994, Appendix 2). The Knowledge Evidence identified here for the supplementation of the Performance Evidence includes an awareness of, for example, the 'defects and dangers that are common across the given range for the element of competence', and 'principles of earthing and bonding', very clear illustrations, it would seem, of the inclusion of knowledge with the practical skills, and on the face of it (admittedly to a non-specialist) an appropriate background to the performance requirements.

It is certainly to be hoped, given the safety-critical nature of the operations that are described in this Unit, that in practice very careful precautions are taken to ensure that knowledge and skill are in full mutual support; and perhaps this evidence really does confirm that this is the case; yet, looking a little further, one still finds grounds for disquiet. It is one thing to itemise what people should know or understand, in order to carry out a given procedure safely on different occasions, but it is also extremely important to document the manner in which that knowledge will be assessed. The 'knowledge' samples provided by NCVQ, while being in some respects reassuring, at the same time contain characteristics that cast doubt on the adequacy of what is being achieved.

The problem is this: the NCVQ Statement (p5) quotes the Electrical Contractors' Association as responding to the Smithers Report, 'There will be written examinations and practical skill tests', and this is comforting. If, however, we turn to another example provided and tested, we come upon an interesting formula. A doctrine, as it were, of implicitness is invoked: if someone can carry out the approved procedure, then it can safely be assumed that they do in fact have the relevant knowledge and understanding. Let us take the case, provided by NCVQ, of a Unit in Pensions Administration at Level IV (Appendix 5). For Element 7.2 of Unit 7, the prescribed Knowledge and Understanding here is at first sight impressive and wide-ranging. It entails the ability to refer to a number of Statutory Instruments, and, in addition, to 'other Acts, Memoranda and Statutory Instruments which amend this framework from time to time'. This must surely count as knowledge; yet it is unclear what evidence is specified to indicate that this knowledge and its proper deployment has been understood. We are told that:

> Letters which meet all the performance criteria and which concern benefits payable under one type of scheme, provide sufficient evidence to infer competence in other types of schemes in that range, and possession of the underpinning knowledge and understanding (NCVQ 1994, Appendix 5).

This illustrates the principle of 'implicitness'; and it seems to take away with one hand much of what is being given by the other. If there is no thorough and obligatory independent testing of knowledge and understanding; if these elements may be inferred from a sample of what the learner does; then, however fully the knowledge itself may be specified, everything continues to turn on matters of interpretation regarding how much, exactly, is implicit. There is an uncomfortable and potentially dangerous ambiguity present in the design of Units that, apparently, allows any of the lists of understandings to be identified as present on the basis of pure observation: just how much discretion do individuals have to infer what is implied? Are we talking of electricity here, as well as of the payment of benefits?

'Implicitness', it could be argued, is a slippery slope. True, provision is made for numerous supplementary methods of assessment. In Level III Plumbing Unit (NCVQ 1994, Appendix 3) reference is made to oral assessment, multiple choice tests, short answer tests or written assignments. Further, the NCVQ rejoinder (p4) observes that the separate assessment of knowledge is unequivocally required. This claim is supported by the guideline:

> .... where performance evidence alone is limited and does not permit reliable inference of the possession of necessary knowledge and understanding, this must be separately assessed.

These are, clearly, well-intended words; but they seem to introduce another layer of subjectivity into a system whose chief claim to distinction rests on its capacity for producing objective judgments. As in the old philosophical example, we all know that liberty and licence are not the same thing; the real difficulty arises, not in assenting to some such truism, but in deciding what constitutes each of these in a given situation. When is enough, enough? When is the opportunity for inference from a performance an adequate one? Simple stipulation about written tests being used as appropriate rings as hollow as the pieties of any other voluntary code, and reflects what is arguably a deep (if selective) ideological commitment on the part of NCVQ to laissez-faire practices.

The above comments are based upon material provided specifically by NCVQ in response to the Smithers Report, to support NCVQ's argument that knowledge and understanding are not lacking in NVQs. We are not totally convinced by this evidence - if anything, its impact is somewhat alarming since, where one might expect to find a rationale, one is offered a mass of examples: as though the invocation of knowledge could guarantee its presence. Of course, verifiers and assessors are intended to provide effective cross-checking of the quality of learning. Even these safeguards, however, are open to question and will be considered below.

The evidence offered by NCVQ, then, seems to permit a good deal of latitude to individual users and writers of Units. We might compare this with the situation described by Professor Smithers in his chapter on European Solutions. We need not necessarily go all the way with the German approach, whose apprentice plumbers 'must sit four major written examinations and two long practical examinations' (p26). Nonetheless, such an emphasis on understanding and knowledge, with little left 'implicit', is clearly very different from the NCVQ model and might well be preferred by some people as tending to reduce ambiguity and confirm capacity: ironically, twin aims of the NCVQ's programme.

To this may be added the consideration that, traditionally, a large part of education has been involved in making the implicit, 'explicit'. That is, it has required of people that they put into words their reasons for doing those things which they might do more or less automatically, eg, providing a justification for teaching accurate spelling and grammar. In this context, the apparent equivocation over the importance of knowledge, together with its relegation to secondary and supplementary status, begin to seem, by European standards, distinctly quirkish.

Verifiers and assessors have been mentioned above, and of course procedures are built into NVQs that are intended to ensure quality provision. Often these procedures will work well. However, it is arguable that there is a general flaw in the methodology that NCVQ apply to monitoring quality in their Units, and one that is connected with the problem of maintaining standards where the universal base of theoretical knowledge is rendered problematic or secondary. It is, after all, perfectly possible to imagine the best-case scenario for the operation of NVQs, where performance criteria are appropriate, and are fully supported by other kinds of evidence such as written examinations which could provide further assurances of understanding. Such cases will be assessed and verified in depth and, other things being equal, may lead to very satisfactory learning outcomes. When large, well-known companies implement NVQs for example, it is likely that the NVQ framework will lend itself to such purposes: the culture of the company will ensure quality in the training.

There is however an obvious drawback to the approach to monitoring and evaluation that is often favoured by NCVQ: the danger of overlooking negative or, more strictly, unwelcome evidence. The problem may be illustrated like this, given NCVQ's fondness for the driving test analogy: NVQs may be likened to the family car in certain important respects, having to accommodate as it does all kinds of users in all sorts of circumstances. Now although cars may be easy to use, they are not easy to design or build, and one reason for that is that, however well they may work in ideal conditions, for much of the time they will not be driven in such conditions. They need to be, to a considerable extent, foolproof. They must be forgiving of drivers who corner too fast; who use the wrong spare parts, or who neglect to service their vehicles until their efficiency is grossly impaired. The typical car is built, not only for the ultra-careful motorist with very high standards, but also for other users who may, as we all know, have different driving habits. It follows that testimonials from the ideal motorist may not, sadly, be as significant as testimonials from those who, without assistance from anti-lock braking systems, might have wrapped the car around a lamp-post. For this reason, testimonials to the value of NVQs from Glaxo, or Conoco, or Comet such as NCVQ (1994, p3) provide, while heartening, are not surprising. The in-built expertise of such companies will ensure that NVQs stay on the road and even perform like a Rolls-Royce. The question is, however, what happens when smaller organisations with less sophisticated training infrastructures drive the same vehicle? Is quality assurance built into NVQs, or is their quality dependent upon that of the user? To what extent will the system prevent the user from adapting it to the point where the training becomes inadequate? That is the real quality-control question that should be asked, not one about how good NVQs may be in ideal conditions.

An alleged example, pointed out to us by lecturers involved in construction industry training, may help to illustrate this point. In 1992, the Construction Industry Training Board and City and Guilds jointly issued Competence Requirements for Bricklaying Level III (CR 027/3). It was intended that these should include some vehicle for recognising supervisory experience on the part of candidates and, to this end, Uni No D 32 (09/91) was incorporated. The only difficulty with this arrangement was that the Unit of Competence D32 was actually entitled: Assess Candidate Performance; the means of providing, and recognising, the above-mentioned 'supervisory experience' entailed candidates assessing one another's portfolios and having this accredited as appropriate experience to fulfil the requirements of the Unit. A harmless enough procedure, it might be thought - except that it would have eventuated in 18 year old trainees being certified as trained assessors! The Unit was withdrawn in this context, having been criticised as unworkable by the intended deliverers; had this view not prevailed, assessor status would have been granted as a kind of trivial by-product of a quite different kind of activity: a symbolic representation, perhaps, of the importance accorded to the extensive professional expertise and experience of qualified teachers. Where such situations can arise, it is not unreasonable for the as yet unconvinced, if sympathetic, onlooker to continue withholding judgment on NCVQ's quality control procedures. And all this is to say nothing of the numerous allegations (eg, Observer 15/6/94) of intense pressure in colleges to pass NVQ candidates, regardless of their real achievements.

We can reflect on this question further, in the light of the evidence provided in the Report from the Institute of Manpower Studies on NVQs in the Construction Industry: 'Will NVQs Work?' (Callender 1992). In addition to reviewing the evidence provided by her, and relating it to what has been said about NCVQ's arguably somewhat laissez-faire requirements concerning the testing of knowledge, some points of a general nature will be made that suggest just how a system of training may perform when a worst-case scenario is enacted, as opposed to a best-case one. General issues of quality control are raised by the above-mentioned IMS Report and it is clear from this document that parts of the construction industry do not operate in the same way as a large multinational company. Rather, it

is a national industry. Its workforce is highly mobile and fragmented, unlike many other industries. Its manpower and training requirements within a given locality are difficult to predict and are determined primarily by large building projects. These have a limited life and it is unlikely that TECs will be able to respond fast enough to meet the construction industry's training demands in their area. (p16)

In short, a situation is outlined where summary 'on-the-job' training and assessment are difficult and sometimes less than satisfactory. A number of problems arising from attempts to assess at the workplace are highlighted (p23), including issues concerning completeness of exposure to learning situations, mobility of labour, health and safety questions, the logistics of building, and the prevalence of teamwork. In National Vocational Qualifications and Further Education (Bees and Swords 1990, p194) Roy Boffy makes similar points, though from a standpoint sympathetic to the general idea of work-based learning

> One of the major concerns with NVQs at present is that conditional accreditations are running well ahead of the technical work that needs to be done to support them.

It may be that, in the light of the problems mentioned above, this is a situation endemic to certain industries, or parts of industries where these areas suffer from the same limitations in terms of fragmentation. NCVQ need to be clear, and candid, on the extent of such difficulties though.

However (and here we come to one of the more intriguing conceptual issues in the whole discourse of 'competence', the 'employment-led curriculum' and so on), workplace assessment is dear to the heart of NCVQ because it 'offers the most natural form of evidence of competence and has several advantages, both technical and economic' (Department of Employment/NCVQ 1991, p21). 'Natural' is a key word here; it is echoed in the frequent use of the idea of 'naturalistic' assessment to describe the processes of assessment thought to be the most appropriate and relevant to the testing of occupational competence. It is a word much favoured for its persuasive force and, by the same token, one that should not be allowed to pass unscrutinised. An examination of the idea will also serve as a lever to shift the discussion back, finally, to a deeply contentious aspect of the views expressed in the Smithers report.

The fact is that we live in a world of highly contrived activity where 'naturalness' is neither easy to identify nor, if identified, necessarily desirable or appropriate. In both philosophical and practical terms, what is 'natural' is highly problematic: to talk of what is 'natural' is not simply to describe a state of affairs but, rather, to commend one. It is not natural, for example, to take awkward and cumbersome safety precautions when carrying out tasks on a building site; but, no doubt partly as a result of this perfectly natural reluctance, the construction industry has a high accident rate. The same kind of argument can be applied to the use of the term 'realistic' in the appraisal of work-based learning situations; the practices evident on site or at work are not always those that would or should be taught to trainees; and the 'real', or 'proper', way of doing something may not be the same as the 'actual', let alone the 'natural' one. Of course, there is no substitute for hands-on experience; but questions of what should be learned, and when, should not be swept aside with gestures towards some 'natural' state of affairs that merely represents the speaker's own prejudices. And, for those who might regard such points as mere philosophers' quibbles, Argyle's (1972) work demonstrating, for example, how industrial supervisors' performance tends to worsen with time and with experience, might inject some seriousness into the issues.

It may not be too fanciful to assert, in fact, that one way of characterising the NCVQ approach to learning might be as representing the arrival in its latest reincarnation of the 'naturalistic curriculum'. An emphasis on the 'real world'; a mistrust of theory; the cardinal value placed on 'experience': all recall, and perhaps unconsciously derive from, wider streams of naturalistic theory represented, for example, by the work of Jean-Jacques Rousseau (1762). He tells us:

Give your scholar no verbal lessons; he should be taught by experience alone;

and

We, who only give our scholars lessons in practice .... prefer to have them good rather than clever. (pp56, 66)

These injunctions come from him, not from an NCVQ document. The philosophies involved are clearly not so far apart as might have been imagined, however.

Rousseau's paradox, and the problem that he wrestled with in various ways, was that of having to manipulate Nature so that she did not, disobligingly, teach the wrong things. A pragmatist can cheerfully manage such a situation perhaps; a philosopher like Rousseau, wedded to consistency as a philosopher must be, finds such contradictions deeply embarrassing. The contradictions are still present: would that NCVQ were more embarrassed by them!

All this returns us to the issue of student-centredness raised by Smithers as a supposed weakness of the NCVQ approach. He has clearly identified something that is amiss in their shifting of the onus of responsibility from tutors to teach, to students to claim credit via portfolios. Nonetheless, it is not, in the end, at all helpful of him to criticise NCVQ in such terms - any more than it is to commend a particular approach as 'natural'. What is helpful is to pick out exactly where a given approach goes wrong, or otherwise. To have analysed the NCVQ model in terms of a particular, pathological, version of 'student-centredness'; one heavily reliant on the sort of 'naturalistic' elements identified above, reinforced with the language of student 'empowerment', would have taken us forward in this particular respect. What has actually happened is that the legitimate aims of student-centredness have been thrown out with the dubious bathwater of some NCVQ practices; while Smithers has been put into a situation of defending written examinations as the obvious alternative to the competence model - and being characterised as 'prescriptive' for his pains.

It will be sad if the real gains represented by student-centred learning are to be devalued and dismissed by becoming associated too firmly with NCVQ models. And this danger points up a need which might perhaps have been met more adequately in the Smithers Report. To have identified a version of student-centred learning that offers the academic rigour Smithers (rightly) demands without losing the benefits of the more open system that NCVQ has arguably, other things being equal, made possible: this would have been a synthesis eminently worth attaining and, in the view of many who believe in the immense value of student-centred learning properly conducted, one possible of attainment. Perhaps it was no part of Smithers' brief to offer such a synthesis; it is unfortunate, however, that his Report may, in this respect, tend to perpetuate a somewhat regressive dichotomy.

Where then does this leave us? On the one hand, the NCVQ model has achieved a good deal in a short space of time, and there is much within it that is innovative and developmental. It is our contention, however, that the approach embraces a number of fundamental conceptual difficulties, particularly those involving the relationship between competences and underlying knowledge. Somewhat disturbingly, the very rebuttals offered by NCVQ of the criticisms raised in this area tend to augment, rather than allay, the doubts of critics; for whom what appears to be equivocal and ambiguous language seems to reappear at every turn. While of the Smithers Report, it may be said that it has promoted a debate of some value and raised decisive questions on the same topics; while incidentally accelerating the process of NCVQ's amplifying and justifying their approach to training. If Smithers had been less sweeping about 'student-centredness', a possible negative impact on the use of innovative methods might have been avoided; but the issue has been flagged up and the hope is that it can be worked through with an increasing conceptual clarity. This paper is intended to contribute in some small degree to that important aim.

References

Argyle, M. (1972), *The Psychology of Interpersonal Behaviour.* Hardmondsworth, Penguin Books.

Boffy, R. (1990), Occupational Competence and work-based learning - the future for Further Education? in Bees, M. and Swords, M. (eds) *National Vocational Qualifications and Further Education.* London: Kogan-Page/NCVQ.

Callender, C. (1992), *Will NVQs work?* IMS Report No 228. University of Sussex/Employment Department Group/IMS.

Department of Employment (1991), *Guide to National Vocational Qualifications.* London: NCVQ.

Institute of Training and Development/Thames Valley University (1992), *Assessment of NVQs and SVQs.* London: ITD/TVU.

NCVQ (1994) A Statement on 'All Our Futures: Britain's Education Revolution', a Channel 4 Dispatches Programme on 15 December 1993 and associated Report by the Centre for Education and Employment Research, University of Manchester. London: NCVQ.

Polanyi, M. (1958), *Personal Knowledge.* London: Routledge and Kegan Paul.

Pursaill, J. (1989), *National Vocational Qualifications and Further Education.* London: FEU

Rousseau, J.J. (1762 edn.), Emile (Tr B Foxley, 1991) Everyman. London: J M Dent.

Smithers, A. (1993), *All Our Futures: Britain's Education Revolution.* London: Channel 4 Television.

6 Competence in initial teacher-training: technical or professional?

Bob Butroyd

Abstract

The introduction of competence-focused school-based training for secondary school initial teacher-training raises a number of issues for those involved. Foremost amongst these issues is the determination of the nature of competence and the opportunities this provides for course design. This article explores interpretations of competence, models of teacher education, and the application of Social Market principles to education. Social Market philosophy is an important current in Government thinking on education. The possible implications of this approach for teacher education are then examined before the writer offers a view of teacher education which encourages teachers' professional judgment and promotes teacher autonomy.

Introduction

It is not the purpose of this paper to establish the strategic nature of educational reform since 1988. What this paper sets out to do is to explore competence, as published in DFE Circular 9/92, Initial Teacher Training (Secondary Phase), in the context of Social Market philosophy.

For the purposes of this paper the writer uses 'professional' to mean a practitioner of an occupation who is dependent upon advanced learning for the conduct of that occupation. In addition the 'professional' has some degree of control over the quality of the practitioners and the aims of the occupation. 'Technician' is used in the sense of someone skilled in a particular art or craft, but who as a member of that occupation has no control of either the quality of those practising that art or craft, or the aims of its work.

The Social Market philosophy, as described by Skidelsky (1989), promotes the idea that freedom, within the area of social provision, is increased by the dispersal of power. Power is defined as the ability to act. Competition reduces the power of organisations. Competition increases the power of the consumer through choice, and this choice is better expressed through 'the right to exit'. In educational terms this would mean ultimately some form of voucher system whereby the consumer/parent would have the right to spend the voucher at one of a range of competing educational organisations.

Davis (1993) further develops a Social Market perspective on education. Although recognising that schools are not supermarkets, he feels that the market forces which determine the development of supermarkets should shape the provision of education. The role of government is to guarantee the overall funding of education, as well as force schools to provide information for this market. The government should not determine the curriculum; there should be different curriculum provisions provided by different providers. As far as Davis is concerned government legislation has not gone far enough in this respect.

Circular 9/92 brought about three major reforms for the Initial Teacher Training (ITT) of secondary school teachers:

i) schools should play a much larger role in ITT as full partners of higher education institutions (HEIs).
ii) the accreditation criteria for ITT courses should require HEIs, schools and students to focus on the competence of teaching.
iii) institutions, rather than individual courses, should be accredited for ITT (DFE 1992, p1).

In order to explore competence this paper examines current views on school-based training, for it is the school that plays a pivotal role in teacher training. The next section looks at the different models of competence in the context of 9/92. The circular itself, so this paper contends, allows Higher Education Institutions (HEIs) and schools to go beyond the behaviourist interpretation of competence. The third section then summarises the major philosophies and models of teacher education in order to put the 9/92 changes in perspective.

Although the final section places the development of competence-based training within Social Market philosophy, it offers an alternative development of competence-based training, grounded in professional judgment and a regard for the hermeneutic, or reflective practitioner philosophy of teacher education.

School-based training

There is an apparent agreement across the political spectrum about the need for more school-based training. Shaw (1992) identifies O'Hear and Hargreaves along with Warnock as people who favour more school-based teacher training. Hargreaves et al advance the idea of teaching schools along the lines of teaching hospitals. They feel that to simply consider the amount of time the trainee is based upon school premises is to misunderstand the real issue. They consider that it is far more important that the school takes the leading responsibility for initial training, and that they receive all of the funding currently available for the trainee. Making the school the lead body, rather than equal partner with the HEI, would help the integration of theory and practice; the real issue according to Beardon, Booth, Hargreaves and Reiss (1992). The role of HE would be to supply learning packages for teacher-training, which would then be administered by the school. This would free HE to carry out research and development work with experienced teachers.

O'Hear has not made clear his vision of the role of HE in teacher training. However, he does have a very clear view of what he terms education.

> A simple argument is often used by those in colleges and departments of education who wish to preserve their monopoly on the supply of teachers. Teaching is a profession. No professional admits people without professional training. Therefore teachers must have professional training.
>
> As it stands the argument is quite persuasive. Doubts begin to arise when it becomes clear that what is envisaged is training in the subject called 'education' rather than expertise in the subject that the would-be teacher is to teach. A teacher who is innocent of 'education' is said to be unqualified and, hence, unprofessional. (O'Hear 1991, p25)

There seems to be an assumption throughout the article that not only is education separate, or even irrelevant to teaching and learning, but that it takes place exclusively in HE

> The ability to put over a subject is not some further bit of knowledge over and above one's subject. Even allowing that there is a subject called education, studying it would not by itself enhance one's ability to teach ..... How does one learn to teach effectively? Everyone involved in the sometimes bigger disputes about teacher-training seems to agree that the key component is practice. This is hardly surprising since teaching is fundamentally a practical activity. (O'Hear 1991, p25)

His assertion that the study by trainee teachers of 'education' is in itself of little value (and by implication time spent in HE) was not borne out by HMI (1993) in their study of the 'New Teacher'.

> Good depth of knowledge was not by itself enough to ensure successful lessons. There were several instances of secondary teachers with considerable subject knowledge teaching unsatisfactory lessons. For example, a specialist modern language teacher with a Year 7 class failed to motivate the children and lost control of the lesson as a result of not consolidating prior learning before introducing more advanced ideas. (HMI 1993, p7)

At the same time Marks (1992) was trying to undermine the idea that teaching and learning benefited from group work and smaller classes, ideas which were viewed as springing from the 'educational establishment' of which the training colleges were presumably a part. Interestingly Marks was to be co-opted onto the National Curriculum Council and O'Hear onto the Council for the Accreditation of Teacher Education (CATE). Both were to serve on the School Curriculum and Assessment Authority (SCAA).

The Hillgate Group (1989), of which Marks is also a member, and Sheila Lawlor (1990) had between them orchestrated an attack upon higher education involvement in ITT. Lawlor favours abolition of the PGCE and the BEd and the Hillgate Group promotes a version of the Licensed teacher route, which they called the 'apprenticeship route', although this would be provided alongside other routes.

At the other end of the political spectrum Dave Hill (1991), of the self-styled 'radical left', put this forward from the Hillcole Group as a recommendation to a future Labour Government:

> Whatever models of teaching practice/school experience are used, ITE courses should become substantially school-focused, with students spending more time in schools. (Hill 1991, p28)

Shaw (1993) suggests that some schools, particularly those in the Oxford University scheme, which already had a more equal partnership in the training of teachers, were finding benefits from students' longer attachments.

Furlong (1988) claimed that Higher Education was having equally positive experiences.

> The length of the school attachment was justified not only on the grounds that it allowed the student the maximum possible time in which to acquire professional skills. An extended placement also generated a substantial amount of material - that is, situations and problems which students had

experienced - to be subjected to review and analysis. This material formed the basis for the development of grounded theory. Additionally it was through the concurrent alternating structure of the school attachment and time spent in the university that a creative and interactive relationship between the specifics of practice and the generalisations of theory was achieved. (Furlong 1988, p68)

Earlier research work on the PGCE at Huddersfield University (Butroyd 1993) identified the importance of the school experience to the trainee teachers.

Many mature entrants to higher education have specific vocational goals. For some students the teaching and learning styles experienced during previous academic, vocational and work-based study may not prepare them for the demands of teacher training and teaching itself.

School experience can play a leading role in promoting teaching and learning styles appropriate to the trainee teacher. (Butroyd 1993, p54)

However, a simple increase in the time spent on school premises is not sufficient in itself to ensure maximum advantage from the school based experience.

'mere activity' at the workplace does not constitute experience ..... from the perspective of learning through experience, learning is not to be conceived in terms of its outcome ..... Instead, learning is to be conceived as a continuous process which is grounded in experience. Consequently ..... when considering the validity of assessments of work-based learning, one must consider not only the assessment of learning outcomes but also the assessment of the learning process and *its* validity. (Benett 1993, p87)

Benett (1993) suggests here that the outcomes (competences) are not sufficient as indicators of the quality of learning. The learning process itself needs to be evaluated.

Recent case studies do not indicate that more school-based training necessarily provides the environment for this process. McNamara (1990) quotes from two pieces of research to support this statement. Mansfield, investigating the supervisor's role during teaching practice, claims that even though supervisors in school recognise the importance of critical analysis of lessons this rarely occurred, closer attention being paid to class teaching situations. A study by Calderhead, also in McNamara, followed the students who reached a 'plateau' in their reflective thinking because they were limited by factors in the classroom.

McNamara also sounds a word of warning when he refers to a one-year school-based scheme which was abandoned after the first year.

> The students were placed in an ambiguous position; they were neither students nor 'real' teachers. The demands upon the supervising teachers were such that they felt unable to repeat the experiment. The logistics of running the course were too complex and the students missed the initial security and support of a university-based course. (McNamara 1990, p130)

O'Hear (1988), drawing on what Hill (1991) would call a classroom competency model, is virtually describing an apprenticeship system whereby the teacher will pick up attitudes and the right 'spirit' (the essential ingredient for a 'good' educator) almost by osmosis: the antithesis of the 'reflective practitioner'.

Beardon and Hargreaves et al (1992), in drawing up criteria for a competency approach to teaching, consider two strands of training. One of these strands is subject-specific and the other is concerned with 'professional knowledge'. The success of the trainee would be measured by outcomes. Each trainee would be under the supervision of a mentor and a professional tutor. These two personnel would be responsible for providing the opportunity for the trainee to demonstrate competence. They suggest a breadth of outcomes which include evaluation of teaching, although, as with many competency-based approaches, the processes involved in reaching these outcomes are left undetermined.

Williams (1993) describe three models of mentoring: basic, developed and extended. He suggests that anything less than 'extended mentoring', involving a variety of strategies, discussing and developing teacher/learner ideas, and collaborative teaching, will significantly restrict the development of the trainee teacher.

It is necessary for trainees to be involved in classroom practice. But this is not sufficient. It is important that the trainee has time for, and access to, informed professional opinion, in order to consider and if necessary change her approach to teaching and learning.

As with many initiatives in education, there were many protagonists from a variety of perspectives. By January 1992 the proposals of the Secretary of State could be sure of enthusiasm in some quarters and what might be termed a healthy scepticism in others. He could also be sure of people from different political and professional interests who were prepared to work with the Circular 9/92. It appeared that everybody wished to be involved at the beginning, if only in some cases, to help to determine the nature of the changes rather than see something imposed which was not to their liking.

Competence-based initial teacher-training

Through statements of competence Circular 9/92 describes a 'core' or 'base' from which ITT courses are to develop.

> The statements of the competences expected of newly qualified teachers do not purport to provide a complete syllabus for initial teacher-training. They specify issues on which the case for approval will be considered. It is recognised that institutions are developing their own competence-based approaches to the assessment of students. (DFE 1992, p3)

This statement from 9/92 allows HEIs, in partnership with their schools, a degree of latitude in their interpretation of a competence-based course. Furthermore, the document is not altogether clear about the exact detail of the competences. The circular lists five:

<u>Competences Expected of Newly Qualified Teachers</u>
Subject Knowledge, Subject Application, Class Management, Assessment and Recording of Pupils' Progress, and Further Professional Development. (DFE 1992, Annex p1)

One interpretation of this is to view these headings as the competences, which are supported by 27 criteria, through which the newly qualified teacher might be expected to be able to demonstrate competence. (DFE 1992, Annex p2) An alternative interpretation would be to view 9/92 as presenting 27 specific competences which were to be demonstrated before qualification, grouped under five headings; a view which is far more prescriptive in terms of course design.

According to Hargreaves (Elliot 1993) this ambiguity in government policy is not uncommon. He suggests that governments across the world can be seen to be determining broad educational policy which is then delivered by small units. A framework is provided by government and the provision itself is left to be determined by others. These units are then held accountable for operating within government requirements.

The way in which these competences are viewed is central to an understanding of the options available to those involved in course design. Norris (1991) provides four classifications of competence. Behaviourist constructs of competence are defined in terms of outcome or product. What is to be learnt by the students is to be 'transparent, observable, and measurable .... it is a description of action, behaviour or outcome in a form that is capable of demonstration, observation and assessment'. (Norris 1991, p322)

The generic construct of competence does not, unlike behaviourist constructs, reduce a job into its 'composite knowledge, procedures, skills and tasks' but identifies those competences which distinguish 'expert' from 'average' performers. Generic competences are an aggregation of the constituent parts of these distinguishing competences. They can be identified through interviewing as well as behaviour.

Cognitive constructs concentrate upon identifying the potential of a candidate as distinct from their performance. Potential is dependent upon deep understanding, taking into account fluctuations in the relative importance of certain aspects of the competence, dependent upon circumstances. It is difficult to demonstrate this high level of competence through practice.

Ethnographic accounts of competence stress the influence of: the specific situation, as competent behaviour cannot always be predetermined; the nature of the group assessing the competence, as different interest, client or occupational groups may have different perceptions of competence; the context, as aspects of competence may diminish in importance in different situations.

Norris presents an example of an American researcher, Ralph Tyler, who in 1927 had the task of classifying two million index cards, sent in by teachers, which described their activities. Tyler, in a later interview, had this to say:

> You know about every 20 years or so the uneasy tension between theory and practice in professional education (whether it be doctors, teachers or others) alternates between emphasising the activities within the profession, or emphasising the theory that may help to guide the profession. This was one of those times, when, as now, the emphasis was on finding the competences of teachers and trying to focus on them. (Norris 1991, p338)

Norris's classifications take the notion of competence beyond the NVQ model of outcomes and performance criteria which the behaviourist construct underpins. Benett (1993) argues that workplace based assessment attempts to deal with some very broad areas of learning. This learning is not restricted to those areas that are 'transparent, observable and measurable'.

> If one unpacks what is being assessed at the workplace, one finds it includes components such as practical skills, the application of theoretical knowledge, competence, attitudes, personal development and experience. (Benett 1993, p87)

Behaviourist constructs cannot deal with all of this. Analysis of the competences under the headings of knowledge and application indicate that some have a greater affinity with cognitive competence (see competences 2.1 and 2.3) and generic competence (see competences 2.2, 3.2, 3.3 and 3.4) than behavioural definitions (although 3.1 and 3.5 may be closer to the behaviourist model). There is a danger that providers of ITT may become too concerned with the definitions and limitations of competence. Indeed, as we have already noted, 9/92 recognises the limitations of being too prescriptive with a competence-based approach.

The CNAA (January 1992) report on competence development in ITT illustrated a variety of approaches from institutions and came to this conclusion:

> The distinction between narrow behavioural objectives-based definitions of competences and the broader definitions which encompassed knowledge, understanding and attitudes was noted. It was felt that the use of competence-based approaches should sharpen the focus of teacher education but care should be taken to ensure that such an approach did not narrow the curriculum or detract from the importance of cognitive and affective factors. (CNAA 1992, p26)

Even an assumption of 27 competences, as opposed to 5, supports the view that the 9/92 competences do not have to restrict achievement of competence to a box-ticking exercise. The wording of the '27' would certainly allow a generic, or even cognitive interpretation of competence (although I am less certain of allowances for the ethnographic construct).

Competence-based training is widespread throughout the 'professions' in the UK: Police Officers, Accredited Social Workers and Nurses are amongst those whose training is competence-based. The competences of 9/92 continue within this pattern, although they differ markedly in one respect: they are not as prescriptive and limiting as those which lay down outcomes and performance criteria. Norris offers a possible explanation of this:

> To put it bluntly there is a massive mismatch between the appealing attraction of precision that surrounds competency or performance-based programmes and the imprecise, approximate and often arbitrary character of testing when applied to human capabilities. (Norris 1991, p336)

William Taylor (1991), Chair of the Council for the Accreditation of Teacher Education (CATE), whilst subscribing to the view that competence ignores the 'messy reality', feels that there is scope for an interpretation of competence in teacher education that can take into account the 'strategic thinking' required of a teacher. He continues:

.... the most effective means of ensuring skill transfer is for 'knowing how' (technique) to be properly underpinned by 'knowing why' (reflection). The language has changed over the years, but teacher educators have always argued that effective performance rests on the interplay of practice and reflection, a position in which they are currently sustained by the Secretary of State's Criteria. (*Criteria referred to were those of Circular 24/89, criteria replaced by Circular 9/92*)

.... The short term demonstration of behavioural competence is not, however, an adequate substitute for participation in well-designed formal study programmes. As the writings and ideas of Oakeshott, Polanyi and others make clear, classroom skills are a necessary but not sufficient condition for the proper exercise of a teacher's responsibilities. (Taylor 1991, p57)

Alexander and Judy (1988) offer an insight into the complexities of the strategic thinking required of the teacher with a review of literature which examines the nature of domain-specific and strategic knowledge. They describe three classifications of domain-specific knowledge: Declarative Knowledge, which is factual information, or knowing what: Procedural Knowledge, which consists of functional units of knowledge with domain-specific strategies, which enable someone to know how, and Conditional Knowledge, which involves knowing when and where to use the other forms of knowledge.

In addition, the strategic thinking of procedural knowledge can be restricted to one domain (eg, identification of a statement of fact or opinion in History), or can be general (applying the same procedures for identifying opinion or fact in Economics, Law, Physics etc). Enabling the learner to develop these forms of knowledge is further complicated by the fact that the teacher is also a learner and will herself be engaged in the selection of the appropriate procedures for her own development as a teacher trainee. This whole development would be very difficult to track in a behaviourist approach to the competence of the teacher.

Demonstration of competence which looked for evidence in a given situation may not take account of its 'informed' or 'intelligent' execution. An example would be 2.3.1 (DFE 1992, Annex p2) 'produce coherent lesson plans which take account of NCATs and of the school's curriculum policies'. Isolating this 'competence' and recording its demonstration risks taking the lesson plan out of context (ie, can a lesson plan be coherent if it cannot be implemented, possibly because it failed to take into account some of the other 'competences'?)

If 9/92 is to be interpreted as 27 separate competences, then this atomisation may not enable the assessor of the trainee to identify a competent teacher. Alexander and Judy describe a situation which those involved in teacher education might do well to heed. It was witnessed by Schoenfield when watching students working on calculus.

Some of these students may have actually solved the given problem, but the time and effort required to do so negatively affected overall task performance ..... it was not necessarily what content or strategy these learners brought to the task, but what they did with that knowledge that counted. What distinguished between success and failure for these students was that the unsuccessful problem solvers spent much more of their time doing, rather than thinking. It may also be the case that some learners approach a given task with a preconceived or biased notion as to what strategy would be appropriate. Based on only a limited understanding of the task and a superficial search of solution paths, they frequently initiate strategic processes that lead them on wild goose chases. (Alexander and Judy 1988, p390)

Bennett et al (1984), in a study of Primary classes, found that 40% of the tasks set for 'high attainers' were too easy, leading to pupils being assigned far too many 'practice' tasks, to the exclusion of other forms of task. Similarly, it was found that 44% of the tasks set for 'low attainers' were too difficult. Bennett et al suggest how to address this difficulty.

In order for adequate diagnosis and explanation to be afforded by teachers additional knowledge and skill in curriculum content areas, and in interacting with individual pupils, is required. Teachers need to be knowledgeable about schemes available, their differing content, assessment procedures and implications for the management of learning. Crucially they need knowledge of how a wide range of pupils typically respond to this content, their common errors and misconceptions. On the basis of such knowledge they need to develop a range of strategies to overcome them.

Attention needs to be drawn to the cognitive complexities of content, rather than concern with mechanical progress; and to the processes whereby pupils arrive at products, rather than to the products themselves. In order to fulfil this change in focus, skills require developing in diagnostic interviewing and the phrasing of explanations. The problems experienced in this study provide a guide in this area although it is likely that training at pre-service level may not meet these same issues. (Bennett et al 1984, pp220-221)

This analysis, and presentation of a solution to the problem of setting inappropriate tasks, demonstrates two things. The first is the interrelated nature of the many complex skills required by the teacher to address just one of the criteria, 3.3:

Set appropriately demanding expectations for pupils.

Secondly, it shows the interrelated nature of the criteria. There is a need to draw upon at least these two other criteria, 3.4 and 3.5, in order to satisfy 3.3.

Employ a range of teaching strategies appropriate to the age, ability and attainment level of pupils. (3.4)
Present subject content in clear language and in a stimulating manner (3.5)

If we treat the 27 statements as competences, or as performance criteria used to demonstrate the competence achieved, then we run the risk of a behaviourist interpretation of the competences which will fail to take into account the very complex nature of the processes in which the trainee is involved, both as learner and as teacher. Use of the five statements of competence would help to avoid the atomisation of the assessment process by recognising the integrative and dependent nature of many of the 27 statements. For example: is it possible to achieve competence in statement 5.3

Assess and record systematically the progress of individual pupils

if there isn't competence in 5.4:

Use such assessment in their teaching.

at the same time?

Similarly is it wise to assess these competences without taking into account the reasons for assessing pupils' work?

Demonstrate they can understand the importance of reporting to pupils on their progress and of marking work regularly against agreed criteria. (5.5)

Reference has already been made to the interrelationship of the criteria regarding the 'coherent lesson plan' and other subject application criteria and a similar case could be made out for others in the 27 criteria. If we don't take account of the strategic thinking required by teachers, then we may develop an ITT scheme which does not develop this crucial skill and therefore diminishes the nature of the teacher's role.

Because teaching and learning are complex, as with pupils, it does not mean that they cannot be assessed. The procedures for assessment are difficult to specify but it can be done; it is the fragmentation of assessment, a disregard for the interrelated nature of many of the elements of teaching and learning, which can make a nonsense of the assessment process and an ITT course.

Models of teacher education

The 1980s have seen the development of a number of entry routes to Qualified Teacher Status (QTS). These will be briefly described later on. However, to make sense of these developments, this section will look first at the philosophies underpinning these routes.

Elliott (1993) describes three basic philosophies of teacher education. The Platonic, or rationalist, view of the teacher has perhaps been the dominant one for the past 30 years. This view of teacher education places the initial phase firmly in higher education, where theories of educational practice are taught. These theories are then applied during a teaching practice. Subsequent to qualification the teacher's first appointment would involve a probationary period in order to act as a safety net. Subsequent professional development would be determined by the individual teacher on the basis of professional needs determined by herself/himself.

Those who subscribe to the Social Market (*see the next section for a further development of this*) view teaching as the demonstration of practical skills. Teacher education becomes teacher training, and because of its inherently practical nature should be based in the school.

> From the social market perspective the initial training phase constitutes induction. It need not take very long because from this perspective people can identify a few basic behavioural skills which are sufficient to assure the organisation that the trainee is able to function within it. (Elliott 1993, p17)

After qualification it is the senior staff of the school who will determine the future training needs of the Newly Qualified Teacher (NQT), in accordance with the demands of the school development plan.

The third view which gained further prominence through the work of Schon (1983) was the hermeneutic model: teacher education as a practical science. This highlights the teacher's role as researcher. Teaching is viewed as a complex, unpredictable process which requires understanding of the practical situation. Practice is informed by theory, and theory is modified by practice. This is Schon's reflective practitioner. Continued 'Inset' is on the basis of many of the current master degrees for school teachers, involving school-based research, selected by the individual teacher.

There are four main routes to Qualified Teacher Status (QTS) in England and Wales. The most important routes in terms of recruits are the PGCE, with 11,900 entrants in 1990, and the BEd with 11,800 entrants. Both of these routes to QTS have moved from the rationalist to the hermeneutic model. This was happening throughout the 1980s and was encouraged by the introduction of Circular 24/89 (DES 1989). This circular specified a minimum of 75 days' teaching practice on all courses of less than 3 years' duration (100 days for four-year courses) and the additional requirement that there should be a

Practical classroom experience in the first term of a course. (DES 1989, p7)

These changes encouraged the testing of theory in practice, and the modification of theory in the light of experience. However, three years later 9/92 pushed the PGCE and, in some institutions, due to the accreditation of institutions instead of courses, the BEd into the Social Market model. This is a model of competence which has an emphasis upon basic skills and is developed through school-based work.

The other two major routes, although numerically less significant, are important politically, as they are models for current and future development. The Articled Teacher scheme with its first full intake of 403 in September 1990 is perhaps the model for the 9/92 PGCE. Based upon Postgraduate entry it specified that 80% of the time of the entrant should be spent in the school, with 20% of the time based in HE. Indeed a number of the 27 'competences', or criteria, can be found in circulars 18/89 and 24/89 which relate to the Licensed and Articled Teacher Schemes.

The Licensed Teacher Scheme, introduced in 1989, relies upon non-graduate entry, with 90% of the time based in school, with recommendation from the headteacher for QTS after the first year if appropriate. A less 'restricting' version of this is the model for the Hillgate group. This group would like to see headteachers and governors appoint 'anybody with suitable knowledge and experience' (Hillgate Group 1989).

Both of these schemes fall within the Social Market philosophy. They increase the choice of routes to QTS, whilst creating a layer of NQTs who have basic classroom survival skills. This new layer would not yet, in Hargreaves' (1990) preferred view, be career teachers. This again increases the 'choice' for the headteacher and governors. They may choose to exit from the market for higher 'quality' career teachers.

The development of initial teacher education within the context of the social market

To talk of a single market for education is a mistake. There are different markets in education (Grant Maintained, CTC, Public, Grammar, Comprehensive, vocational, etc) reflecting the different suppliers and the needs of the different purchasers. Similarly there are different markets for the labour of teachers.These are influenced not just by expertise and experience, but also by geographical and many other social, economic and political factors.

Teachers are involved in two categories of market: the education market in which the suppliers are the schools, and those that consume, who are by and large the parents; the other market is that for the teacher's labour. This market is supplied by the individual teachers who have (in the maintained sector) QTS; and the demand is from the schools. This second market is derived from the first. If there was no demand for education there would be no demand for teachers. This first market, the market for education, determines conditions within the market for teachers.

The market for education is itself subject to pressures from other markets. The pressure from other markets is for a reduction in the costs of production. The education of the workforce of any organisation is a cost. There is pressure for costs to be reduced due in part to increased competition from Europe and, increasingly, other newly industrialised countries. Education is in the process of re-evaluation of its product, in order to cut costs. The derived market for teachers is engaged in a similar process. There is a re-evaluation of the teacher. This leads to an attempt to measure the value of the teacher's contribution. As in other markets the pressure is to revalue downwards.

> Investment in economic calculation and visibility tends to increase during periods of financial restraint (Hopwood 1984). In times of prolonged economic decline or threat there is a much greater emphasis on costs, financial information and on measures of input and output. More often than not an apparent concern for the effectiveness of public services such as education or health masks a more politically sensitive concern for efficiency. Efforts to improve the effectiveness or efficiency of a service are often presented as neutral and uncontroversial technical matters when they really represent certain political priorities as opposed to others. (Norris in Elliot 1993, pp31-32)

For markets to operate, the suppliers (schools) and consumers (parents) need to know the value of the 'product' (ie, Education). The

1988 Education Act has tried to address this.

Knowing the value of its product the school then has to 'cost' its provision in order to take its place as a supplier in the market. A major part of the school's cost is the teacher. Prior to the Teachers Pay and Conditions Act (1991) this was not determined by markets, but by minimum price legislation, imposed through the Burnham Committee. With its abolition and the local management of schools the cost of the teacher has to be determined by markets, but in order to do this the value of the *individual* teacher has to be determined.

Lawn (1991) analyses 'quality' as a method of measuring the value of a teacher. Lawn claims that quality in teaching should be understood as a social construct and to support his thesis he traces its development through various historical stages. Lawn views quality as a relative term which depended upon wider society's notion of the role of the teacher within the social context (eg, in the late nineteenth century a teacher's quality was identified by his/her views on the church, alcohol, personal morals, whereas today it might be determined by a teacher's attitude to 'compensatory education' or development of personal and social skills).

The measurement of 'quality' through skills has not been consistent:

> The idea of skill is not consistently emphasised in defined teacher quality, although when it is it alters considerably between cases. It may be loosely referred to or specified in detail, related to classroom control or to pedagogy and curriculum, assumed to be clearly definable or to be discretionary and 'professional'. (Lawn and Ozga 1986, p73)

The competences (whether they be 27 or 5) could be viewed as an attempt to define the skills of a teacher in order to measure quality and to define the relative values of teachers.

Elliott (1993) puts recent developments in ITT in the context of what Handy (1990) called the 'Shamrock' organisation. In this type of organisation there is a core of well trained individuals who make many of the critical decisions of an organisation. There is a second stratum of semi- or unskilled workers involved in what is deemed 'technical assistance', and finally you have a group of specialists, from other fields of work, who are brought in on short-term contracts to deal with specific tasks.

In Elliott's analysis of Hargreaves' (1990) proposals for teacher education he claims that Hargreaves develops the ideas of the Social Market Foundation more fully than any of the New Right groups. Elliott feels that the New Right see that

Learning to teach is a matter of learning the technical skills which enable individuals to function effectively in the production system of education. (Elliott 1993, p22)

These technical skills are supposed to be all that is required of the new teacher. Then, according to Hargreaves, those selected by the senior staff (those with the Professional Development qualifications) can be trained to do what he terms 'advanced level' after a period of five years. These staff will then enter the world of the 'Career teachers', who are to be supported by the assistant teachers ('unskilled') and the associate teachers (short-term contract, 'basic' teaching skills but with expertise in other areas.)

The relative values of the different qualities of teacher will enable the market to discriminate between the different classifications, but also to discriminate between teachers in the same markets, leading possibly to individually negotiated salaries and conditions of service.

Training envisaged by the New Right would limit the development of skills (Lawlor would abolish the PGCE and BEd) and would deny the possibility in most cases for NQT to develop the use of strategic thinking in their teaching. It would in effect lead to the deskilling of teaching - and a denial of the procedures involved in teaching and learning.

Recognition of the teacher's use of strategic knowledge strengthens the case for NQT involvement in curriculum development; it enhances the standing of the NQT and would diminish the argument of the New Right that there are teachers who do not have invested in them complex and valuable skills built up through a rigorous application of subject knowledge in the context of many variables, including relationships with pupils, teachers and other adults.

The competences of 9/92 can be interpreted in a purely behaviourist manner, along with performance criteria which can lead to a purely technical interpretation of the role of the teacher. However, closer analysis of the operations of the teacher reveals a far more complex situation than can be represented by the technical approach.

Success in a role can depend as much on the chemistry of a particular institution or department as on personal characteristics; philosophers fear that competences offer spurious promise of predictability that ignores the messy realities of contingency and caprice. And members of teachers' trade unions look sourly on the likelihood of dilution presented by a more open, competence-based entry, mourn the death of hopes for a greater self-governing professionalism, and are suspicious about the potential for re-certification and regular post-experience testing and appraisal. (Taylor in Grace and Lawn 1991, p57)

Despite Taylor's fears, the wording of 9/92 does not limit the interpretation of competence to that of the behaviourist. 9/92 can provide the basis for defining the professionalism that teachers yearn for.

Determination of the criteria whereby a trainee satisfies the competence offers the opportunity for the use of professional judgment in the assessment. In order to legitimise this approach to the assessment of trainees ITT courses need to determine the nature of professional judgment, to recognise its structure and to promote it. In this manner teachers can retain their autonomy, and advance the cause of professionalism in teaching.

Failure to recognise the skills of the NQT through an acceptance of an inadequate system of ITT will allow the ideology of the Social Market to reduce education to something resembling a bus with a driver who does not know the route: a haphazard journey caught by the lucky few.

In conclusion, the writer offers some features of a professional judgment model of initial teacher education as a basis for discussion.

> Professional judgment cannot exist in isolation. Practitioners have to be able to exchange views and be informed by them.

> Competence and professional judgment are dynamic. This is recognised by a rigorous and regular re-examination of the underlying values and criteria of these two concepts.

> The assessment of trainee teachers should be undertaken by groups of serving teachers who meet regularly in order to consider the progress of a cohort of trainees and use their professional judgment in assessing the trainees. This professional judgment is based upon values and criteria explicitly identified by the group of teachers.

> The overlapping and interdependent nature of the 27 criteria should be overtly recognised in the assessment. Strategic thinking should be recognised as playing a key role in the teacher's development.

This approach to the assessment of ITT competence recognises the complex nature of the teacher's role. In addition to establishing teacher control over the quality of the new entrant it can indirectly determine the aims of the profession.

References

Alexander, P.A. and Judy, E. (1988), *The interaction of domain-specific and strategic knowledge in academic performance*. Review of

Educational Research, vol 58, No 4.

Ball, S.J. (1990), *Politics and Policy Making in Education: explorations in policy sociology.* Routledge.

Ball, S.J. (1988), *Staff relations during the teachers' industrial action: context, conflict and proletarianisation.* British Journal of Sociology of Education 9 (289-306).

Bash, L., Coulby, D. (1989), *The Education Reform Act: Competition and Control.* Cassell.

Beardon, T., Booth, M., Hargreaves, D.,Reiss, M. (1992), *School-Led Initial Teacher Training: the Way Forward.* University of Cambridge.

Bennett, N., Desforges, C., Cockburn, A., Wilkinson, B. (1984), *The Quality of Pupil Experiences.* Lawrence Erlbaum Associates.

Benett, Y. (1993), *The validity and reliability of assessments and self-assessments of work-based learning.* Assessment and Evaluation in Higher Education, Vol 18, No 2, 1993, pp83-93.

Bierlein, L.A. (1993), *Controversial Issues in Educational Policy.* Sage.

Butroyd, R. (1993), Double Module, Independent Supported Study: *an Evaluation of the Subject Enhancement Needs of Students on the PGCE Technology: Business Studies Course at the University of Huddersfield.* MEd at Manchester University.

Council for National Academic Awards (January 1992), *Competence-based approaches to teacher education: viewpoints and issues.* CNAA.

Council for the Accreditation of Teacher Education (1992), *The accreditation of initial teacher training under circulars 9.92 and 35.92, a note of guidance from the Council for the Accreditation of Teacher Education.* CATE.

Davies, E. (1993), *Schools and the State.* The Social Market Foundation.

Department for Education: *Initial Teacher Training (Secondary Phase).* Circular No 9/92 (June 1992).

Department for Education: *Initial Teacher Training: Approval of Courses.* Circular No 24/89 (1989).

Elliott, J. (1993), *Reconstructing Teacher Education: Teacher Development.* The Falmer Press.

Furlong, V.J., Hirst, P.H., Pocklington, K., Miles, S. (1988), *Initial Teacher Training and the Role of the School.* Open University Press.

Grace, G. and Lawn, M. (eds) (1991), *Teacher Supply and Teacher Quality: Issues for the 1990s.* Multilingual Matters.

Grace, G. (1985), *Judging teachers: the social and political contexts of evaluation.* British Journal of Sociology of Education, 6 (3-16).

Handy, C. (1990), *The Age of Unreason.* Arrow Books.

Hargreaves, D.H. (1990), *Remission on a Life Sentence.* Times Higher Education Supplement, No 933, September 21; 90, p17.

Hargreaves, A. and Fullan, M.G. (1992), *Understanding Teacher*

Development. Cassell.

Harris, N. (1986), *The End of the Third World*. I.B. Taurus and Co Ltd.

HMI (1993), *The New Teacher in School*. Ofsted.

Hill, D. (1991), *What's Left in Teacher Education: Teacher education, the radical left and policy proposals*. Hillcole Group.

Hillgate Group (1989), *Learning to Teach*. Claridge Press.

Kyriacou, C. (1991), *Essential Teaching Skills*. Basil Blackwell.

Labour Party (December 1991), *Investing in Quality: Labour's plans to reform teacher education and training*.

Lawlor, S. (1990), *Teachers Mistaught? Training theories of education in subjects*. Centre for Policy Studies.

Lawn, M. and Ozga, J. (1986), *Unequal Partners: Teachers under indirect rule*. British Journal of Sociology of Education, 7.

Louden, W. (1991), *Understanding Teaching: Continuity and Change in Teachers' Knowledge*. Cassell.

McNamara, D. *Research on Teacher Training in a Changing Society: the case of Britain in the late 1980s,* in Tisher, R. and Wideen, M. (1990) Research in Teacher Education: International Perspectives. The Falmer Press.

MCI (1990), *Crediting Competence*. MCI.

Marks, J. (1991), *Standards in Schools*. The Social Market Foundation.

Marks, J. (1992), *Value for Money in Education*. Campaign for Real Education.

Mitchell, L. (March 1993), *Competence and Assessment*. Briefing Sheet No 8 Employment Department.

NCC (1991), *The National Curriculum and the Initial Training of Student, Articled and Licensed Teachers*. NCC.

Norris, N. (1991), *The trouble with competence*. Cambridge Journal of Education 21, pp331-341.

O'Hear, A. (1988), *Who Teaches the Teachers?* Social Affairs Unit.

O'Hear, A. (19.3.91), The Guardian, p25.

O'Keeffe, D.J. (1990, *The Wayward Elite: a critique of British teacher-education*. Adam Smith Institute.

Shaw, R (1992), *Teacher Training in Secondary Schools*. Kogan Page.

Schon, D. (1983), *The Reflective Practitioner: how professionals think in action*. Basic Books.

Skidelsky, R. (1989), *The Social Market Economy*. The Social Market Foundation.

Taylor, W., *Ideology, Accountability and Improvement in Teacher Education,* in Grace and Lawn (eds) (1991) Teacher Supply and Teacher Quality: Issues for the 1990s. Multilingual Matters Ltd.

Tropp, A. (1957), *The Schoolteachers*. London: Heinemann.

Williams, A. 'Teacher Perceptions of their needs as Mentors in the context of developing school-based initial teacher education', British Educational Research Journal, Vol 19, No 4 (1994).

Wooldridge, A (1990), *Education and the Labour Market*. The Social Market Foundation.

7 Accountability and the professional environment of teachers

Philip Mitchell

Abstract

This discussion considers the tension existing between the notions of an autonomous teaching profession and accountability, particularly in the light of the implications of a market-based accountability resulting from the Education Reform Act 1988. The argument presented is that the tendency to impose more detailed accountability structures by those representing the outside community carries a risk of not merely damaging the effectiveness of teachers as educators but also of eroding the very outcomes, particularly a skilled, productive workforce, which government itself currently desires. The issue of the qualities required in teachers is examined, along with the nature of the environment - an inclusive collegial setting - seen to promote those qualities. This discussion is extended to a consideration of the problem of achieving an appropriate relationship between teachers as professionals and the community entitled to call them to account. It is concluded that this relationship, taking account of the democratic context, must be a two-way process.

Introduction

A principle embedded in eastern European regimes before the collapse of totalitarian communism was that the economic imperative justified curtailment of political freedoms of the kind long taken for granted in the west. The argument, in broad terms, was that uncensored political activity, far from enhancing the quality of life, could only lead to disruption of the means of generating material wealth. Whatever the

87

motives for perpetuating the argument for much of the twentieth century, it has apparently proved an ill fit with reality.

An analogous attitude, however incongruous such a statement may appear in a western context, has come to bedevil English education in the wake of the 'Great Debate' initiated by the then prime minister, James Callaghan, in 1976 and, more particularly, the Education Reform Act (ERA) of 1988. To express the point in general terms: the prevailing view of the 1950s and 1960s that education, largely undefined and unrestrained in terms of central government policy, automatically represents a national investment had come close to being stood on its head by the 1980s, after a Conservative administration had taken office. Traditional education no longer commanded acceptance as a certain route to economic prosperity (Williams 1980, p493). A new view was gaining ground - the meaning of 'education' was in need of severe pruning to make it fit an explicitly functional purpose of producing people with the skills seen to be demanded by the market place. Education from the traditional perspective, most notably in the post-compulsory sector, found itself being shunted towards the category of a luxury. Education, a luxury, was becoming a commodity the nation could not readily afford and while it could be allowed to survive beyond the years of compulsory schooling, even flourish in more affluent quarters, it was becoming the norm that individuals requiring it should shoulder a larger portion of the costs involved.

As for the schools specifically, the concern was, to use the phrase of a former Labour minister of state, Gerry Fowler, one of 'excessive liberalization' producing pupils with

> a range of qualifications which add up to very little as a totality, necessarily leading neither into any defined career structure, nor into any defined course of higher education. (Fowler 1977, p117)

While the national curriculum, emerging some ten years after Fowler's comments, has assumed less of a vocational character than he would perhaps have wished, the outcome in terms of the overall pattern of control has been striking. Birley (p15), writing in 1970 on the British tradition, referred to 'decentralization of administration' and 'grass-roots freedom for teachers to develop their own curricula'. Maclure (1988), surveying the ERA 1988, sets out the current reality:

> The local authority's curriculum role is downgraded. It is the national curriculum which provides the local authority, the governors and the headteacher with their marching orders. (p9)

The direction of change is indicative of the increasing emphasis placed on the accountability of the education service, including the teachers. One might be inclined, and urged, to accept that the framework now in place to ensure the ready implementation of the processes of accountability is simple fact and that to seek the restoration of the teaching environment of the past is futile, if not plain silly. Certainly it is difficult to disagree with Lawton (1989, p41) when (referring to the introduction of a national curriculum) he points out that teachers must make the best of their new legal obligations. The argument advanced here is not that an insistence on accountability is *per se* unacceptable but that to apply the principle of accountability without due regard for the question of the professional environment, including the possible value of a traditional approach to the teacher's obligations, is likely to undermine the effectiveness of the education service in the very sense which current government policy is designed to secure.

Of course, any case for the promotion of the idea of a self-accountable professional environment, whether viewed in terms of individual self-accountability or accountability to other members of the profession, must include a worthwhile attempt to demonstrate any loss likely to be suffered by pupils and students, and to the nation at large, if the conditions for such an environment continue to be eroded. Glancing back to the ethos of the 'golden years' long preceding the Education Reform Act, some might maintain that among attitudes prevailing in schools, colleges and universities of, say, the 1950s and 1960s, there could be found a thick strand of complacency and slackness. For example Capitanchik (1994), describing the approach of 'all too many' university teachers to their so-called academic freedom, mentions turning up late and grading students' work with the minimum of attention. Even if it is accepted that there is more than a grain of truth in such thumbnail sketches of teachers' attitudes, whether in higher education or elsewhere, a fundamental issue remains - what kind of teaching environment is most likely to realise teachers' potential for producing outcomes currently sought by government (in addition to what members of the profession might themselves consider desirable)? Is a (perfectly understandable) concern to minimise inefficiency, lack of commitment and the occasional traces of laziness appropriately expressed in terms of an onslaught against the traditional non-interventionist attitude of society to educational institutions and their teachers? While the case for greater accountability, embracing notions of teachers' performance and competence, has a justifiable claim for attention, this is not seen as the vital consideration here. For the fundamental position advocated, if only tentatively, is that accountability can be injurious, whether imposed high-handedly or in a spirit of moderation, if issues of professional autonomy and a professional culture are simply side-stepped. As the Institute for Public Policy Research has recently suggested:

> Whether the government chooses loose or close control of the framework of education, it will always be the teachers who actually create the quality. That is done through every daily transaction with children and their parents. It springs from the personal commitment, knowledge and skill of each teacher. (IPPR 1993, p72)

The rise of accountability - aided and abetted by the post-Fordist wedge

Accountability is not a recent issue. In English education it has strong roots in the Revised Code of 1862 (Armytage 1964, pp124-5), which solidified the system of payment by results. The theme found fresh expression in developments following Callaghan's Ruskin speech in 1976, a watershed in the growth of central control at the expense of the LEAs and teachers' unions (Salter and Tapper 1981, p223). The culminating point was the 1988 Education Reform Act, setting in place the legislative framework for the exposure of education to the accountability of the market place, which took form in, for example, the introduction of open enrolment and the requirement (reinforced by the Education (Schools) Act 1992) placed on schools to provide information on pupil attainment. As the Parent's Charter (1991) pledges:

> The Government's plans are designed to ensure that you have all the information you need to keep track of your child's progress ... and *compare all local schools*. (p2; italics added)

In 1991 teacher appraisal became a legal requirement. In April 1993, the further education (FE) sector 'caught up' with the schools as a result of the provisions of the Further and Higher Education Act 1992. This ushered on to the stage of further education the Further Education Funding Councils (one for England and one for Wales) with a remit to, *inter alia*, 'promote accountability and value for money' and to 'provide a direct incentive to colleges to expand participation by relating an element of their recurrent funding to actual student enrolments' (FEFC(E) 1992, p32). The Act buttressed this commitment to accountability through the conferment of corporate status on colleges, so that, separated from the fold of local authority control and coherent planning by being transferred to employer-led governing bodies, they would be placed in direct competition with each other (McGinty and Fish

1993, p89). Moreover, given the emergence of local Training and Enterprise Councils, whose establishment was announced in December 1988 and which now provide funding for training through the Employment Department, colleges now find themselves competing for students/ trainees with private training organisations. Central government's commitment to accountability to the market place is underlined, in the case of the FE sector, by the proposal, announced in the White Paper (Cm 1536) of May 1991, that, by 1996, training credits should be made available for all young people leaving full-time education at 16 or 17. The objective, in routing funding through the individual trainee rather than through the provider, is to give the former choice and control. The assumption at the same time is that, because training providers will be paid according to their ability to attract trainees (through their training credits), the quality of training will improve.

Inevitably, the cumulative impact of changes occurring within a relatively short time span has been the generation of tensions within and between educational institutions, or, more accurately, among the teaching and support staff involved. As the local education authority (LEA) slips into the shadows, whether in the context of corporate colleges, schools achieving grant-maintained status or those operating within schemes of delegation, competition will intensify, and the future for some schools is certainly less than promising. As Knight (1993) predicts:

> There is every likelihood that as market forces operate over time, some schools will be locked into a descending spiral of under-funding and deprivation.

Merrick (1994) reports claims made by college principals that schools with sixth forms, understandably anxious to retain potential sixth-formers, have failed to distribute information, despite a new legal requirement to do so, on post-16 opportunities available elsewhere. The future for small colleges in thinly populated rural areas appears less than secure (Jackson 1991), while other colleges, according to a survey carried out by the Times Educational Supplement ('Urge to merge strengthens': 1 April 1994), see mergers as the only hope for survival amidst the pressures of the market place. At the same time there is a glimmer of optimism in Maxwell's finding (1994) that a group of colleges have decided, in the light of one year's experience of corporate status, to share expertise, and so reduce costs, rather than adopt a confrontational stance in their quest for survival.

But whether institutions do battle with each other or link forces in attempting to secure a share of the market, they have been forced to address issues of cost-effectiveness. Difficult choices must be made: for instance on the balance which needs to be struck between promoting an institution's image in the market and making information available to parents and employers in an objective and professionally responsible manner (Maclure 1988, p35); or on the distribution of the budget between books, equipment and teachers' salaries. Because salaries consume more than half of expenditure, and given the particular importance of a swift and flexible response to changing circumstances in the post-16 sector, conditions appear to exist for the emergence of a two-level staffing structure, broadly consistent with a post-Fordist model.

Fordism, based on standardised components and repetitive tasks, represents mechanisation and mass production (Murray 1991, pp57-69). The problem with techniques of mass production is the difficulty of matching demand with output. If under-production occurs, then market opportunities are lost. If, in an attempt to capture a larger share of the market, there is over-production, the manufacturer is left with excess stock and the consequent cost of storage or of disposal at a discount. An incentive to overcome such problems - that is, to move beyond Fordism to post-Fordism - resides in the rising expectations of consumers. The demand is for quality goods, wider choice, rapid supply and constant innovation. The hierarchical structure of the Fordist workplace is forced to give way to a flatter, decentralised flexible pattern of production able to draw on higher-level knowledge and skills within ordinary members of the workforce as well as on the expertise of managers. Rank-and-file workers are transformed into a company investment and as such come to enjoy benefits of the kind (eg, health care and security of employment) traditionally enjoyed by workers in Japanese corporations.

The problem in all this for employers is that, in a keenly competitive environment, investing in a wide base of rank-and-file workers becomes expensive. The solution lies in identifying a core group of employees who, representing an investment by the organisation, enjoy job security, opportunities to enhance their skills and knowledge, and fringe benefits, all of which cease to be available to a larger peripheral group of rank-and-file workers. To apply this post-Fordist outcome - the driving of a wedge into the workforce - to the teaching environment: while a professional core remains, many teachers find themselves relegated to a de-professionalised, or 'proletarianised' category of disempowered employees on a teacher-instructor continuum whose principal function is to execute tasks assigned by management rather than exercise professional initiative and judgement. The plight of this second-tier group is accentuated by the present-day surplus of teachers. The more fortunate achieve redeployment or secure an early retirement package. Redundancy stares at the rest. New entrants scramble for part-time work and short-term (hopefully renewable) contracts.

The scenario facing staff at one college is reported tellingly by Beckett (1993). A new management structure, to facilitate 'a vision for the future', resulted in senior teaching staff having to apply for a reduced number of reconstituted posts.

> Those who were not selected had a choice. They could be made redundant. They could be demoted to ordinary lecturers, with their salary protected for three years, provided there was demand for what they taught. Those over 50 could have early retirement with an enhanced pension.

Interestingly, there are instances of institutions apparently committed to enhancing the position of their teaching personnel as a whole. Hymas (1993) reports on one grant-maintained school in an inner-city location whose governors had devised a pay scheme above nationally agreed limits on the basis that savings could be made in other areas of the school's budget. However, the stated aim of recruiting and retaining better, highly motivated teachers must carry with it the danger of the gain for one group resulting in a loss, in terms of both pay and conditions of service, for others. It is significant that the scheme, in effect paying homage to the philosophy of the market place, was met with a sceptical response by union leaders.

For all the noisy complaints voiced against accountability, the chill winds of market forces and the emergence of a post-Fordist under-class of teachers pressed into obedient and 'competent' performance of closely defined tasks, perhaps there is little or no alternative, it might be suggested, to accepting that the new order is a fact of current political and financial life. After all, since there can be no pot of gold to satisfy the aspirations of all teachers, it is vital that schools and colleges concentrate the limited amount of attractive financial rewards on a privileged core of teacher-managers, if centres of learning are to continue to attract the most capable staff and thereby secure for the community effective programmes of education and training and their own survival as institutions. In any case (so the argument might continue) the calibre of many teachers is insufficient for any attempt to universalise a self-accountable professional environment - a professional culture - to prove itself a worthwhile exercise.

The need for an inclusive professional culture

The first and possibly most obvious criticism that can be levelled against a post-Fordist accountability-laden conception of teaching is that it is divisive. Perhaps objections to divisiveness can be readily countered with the assertion that life is inevitably 'divisive'. Examining boards, interview panels, professional bodies, consumers of services, and the serenaded damsel all in their various ways make their choices, and that those choices may be seen as, and actually be, divisive cannot alter the fact that in the nature of human activity such choices will always be made.

Whatever the truth of the matter, all this is something of a distraction. While there is certainly a case for avoiding divisiveness among teachers (for example in relation to the subjectivity and demoralising impact of performance-related pay), there are, in the context in question, more fundamental issues. What kinds of qualities do we need to cultivate in pupils and students? What kinds of qualities do we need from their teachers? Do students learn passively? Or is it an active process? To use the terminology of Devaney and Sykes (1988, p16), is learning, from the student's standpoint, a matter of consumption or production? From the teacher's perspective, is the task one of 'straightforward delivery' (p20) or leadership? In attempting answers to these questions, Devaney and Sykes highlight such considerations as how best to equip the future workforce, the complex nature of problem-solving and the development of students' critical capacity.

Equipping the future workforce

Successive governments have made reference over many years to the importance of nurturing the skills and qualities necessary to ensure Britain's economic survival. For example a White Paper of 1985 (Cmnd 9482) pointed out that young people

> ... must be given both a firm foundation and a flexible approach to their working lives. Upon this depends our future prosperity and growth, for our lasting resource is the skill and adaptability of our people. (Paragraph 1)

This call for flexibility and adaptability has more recently found expression within the ethos of the enterprise culture, the hallmark of current government thinking. As the Employment Department's document *1990s: the skills decade* states:

> We need a workforce with higher levels of skills and the enterprise and initiative to seize new business opportunities. (1990, p6)

What this means in the educational context is a departure from learner dependence on the teacher, so typical of traditional provision, and total commitment to the idea of the active, responsible learner. This might at first be interpreted as implying much reduced demands on the teacher. But, as Tomlinson and Kilner argue:

> Flexible Teaching is very challenging ... Such approaches are often more demanding of the teacher than traditional methods. In addition to specialist subject knowledge Flexible Teachers will need skills in coordination, monitoring, negotiation, group structuring, resource and personnel management. (p6)

All this suggests a need for a teaching profession *all* of whose members possess knowledge and abilities of a high order, if the whole spectrum of student potential is to be fully realised. In other words, it seems fair to assume that teachers generally need leadership qualities, not merely the lower level skills associated with 'straightforward delivery'.

The complex nature of problem-solving

It is proposed then that, if learners are to become responsible and adaptable, and to exercise initiative, high-level qualities are required of all teachers. These qualities are paralleled by the expertise needed to ensure the acquisition by learners of effective problem-solving skills. But it is the very use of a phrase like 'problem-solving skills' which tends to obscure the abilities demanded of the teacher. In recent years considerable emphasis has been placed on the assumption (and that is what it is, rather than established fact) that skills can be identified as being common to a range of occupations and, as such, can be considered to be *transferable* from one situation to another. Examples of such transferable (also described as *core* or *generic*) skills are communication, numeracy and personal effectiveness. A fundamental criticism levelled against this approach is that it involves isolating the skills in question from the specific contexts in which they are applied, thereby rendering them meaningless. For instance Coffield (1990), examining the notion of 'enterprise', comments that this word means different things according to the particular context:

> ... because one can be enterprising both by making a million before one's fortieth birthday and by shepherding passengers out of a burning aeroplane does not mean that there is a generic skill of enterprise whose essence can be distilled and taught. (Coffield 1990, p258)

Jonathan (1987, p106) addresses the tendency in recent times to demote knowledge in favour of a greater emphasis on the *process* of acquiring problem-solving skills. She argues that such a shift is misconceived. Because young people, after long exposure to a subject-based curriculum, are observed to be incapable of applying their knowledge to the solution of problems, it is assumed, erroneously, that a focus on knowledge is of little or no value. This in fact is, firstly, a response (in a sense justified) to an excessive reliance in the past on rote-learning and, secondly, an over-reaction to the more recent realisation that knowledge is subject to revision. She continues:

> Insight that the learning process is itself important is replaced by the false claim that it is all-important: learning skills are no longer seen as a means of applying and extending knowledge; they are offered as a replacement for it. (p106)

Later she states:

> .... although a knowledge of content - badly taught - is not enough to promote these skills [of problem-solving and critical thinking], they can be neither acquired nor exercised without it. For there is no such thing as 'problem solving' or 'thinking': there is only solving this particular problem, or thinking about this particular matter. Not only is a great deal of relevant understanding required to solve a problem: this understanding is required to recognize that there is a problem in the first place. (p112)

For Devaney and Sykes also (1988, p13) the likelihood is that general problem-solving skills cannot be taught, which points strongly to the conclusion that an extensive knowledge base for all teachers must be the norm. Moreover, an important part of the teacher's role is to develop the critical awareness of students (p16), if the latter are to contribute effectively to a work environment demanding innovation and the production of high quality goods. Thus a high standard of general education (meaning wide knowledge, breadth of perspective and a discriminating mind) must go hand-in-hand with technical competence, if young people's opportunities and hence the nation's - any nation's - economic prosperity are to be properly ensured. The concomitant requirement in teachers is that they all be educated, not that some are merely 'competised' (although this is not to suggest that no emphasis needs to be placed on skills of organisation and presentation in the classroom). To allow any group of teachers to slide into a position of being little more than classroom operatives, charged with a duty to deliver prepacked information, drills and attitudes, would appear seriously inadequate.

Collegiality

Teacher autonomy and collegiality represent two possible perspectives concerning the prescription of limits to accountability (accountability being required by an institution's governors, the local education authority and central government). The expression 'teacher autonomy' is used here in the sense of freedom granted to the individual teacher to exercise her/his own judgement derived from personal expertise and commitment to the ethical norms of the profession. Collegiality can be defined as accountability to fellow professionals within the same school or college or to the profession as a whole. In practice the two notions exist in a symbiotic relationship: the individual teacher draws on the knowledge and experience of immediate colleagues or of the profession generally in order to make informed personal responses to one's professional obligations, while the group is sustained by the contributions of the individuals who form it. It would be doing an injustice to the idea of collegiality, however, to limit a definition to 'internal accountability', as if it functions solely as a buffer between the outside community and the individual teacher, in the sense of shielding the latter from ill-judged lay intrusions into professional activity (or, in a totalitarian setting, in the sense of ensuring strict adherence to the requirements of those exercising ultimate political control). The point is that collegiality also implies a supportive environment for the purpose of empowering the teacher to carry out her/his professional tasks competently.

The research of McLaughlin and Yee (1988) into the working environment of schoolteachers points to some interesting conclusions. A recurring theme in the dissatisfaction expressed by teachers generally centres on the paucity of resources. McLaughlin and Yee (1988, pp30-31) note that a good level of resources, while not unimportant, does not in itself lead to greater professional satisfaction. Frustration was found among teachers benefiting from a 'resource-rich' environment, while teachers forced to make do with a 'resource-slim' situation spoke of their work in enthusiastic terms. Evidently non-material factors provided the key: the sharing of ideas with colleagues and working as a member of a team with a sense of collective responsibility and group purpose. Professional opportunity and satisfaction were also observed to increase where the environment was 'problem-solving rather than problem-hiding' (p36) and 'investment-centred rather than payoff-centered' (p37). In such a setting openness and frankness are the norm, with teachers being encouraged to air problems, seen as the concern of the organisation as a whole, and to experiment and innovate, difficult in a system which applies procedures of summative evaluation and performance-related pay (typifying a 'payoff'-oriented approach). A clear picture emerges from the investigations of McLaughlin and Yee: teachers work effectively as members of a professional group rather than when they are under pressure to comply with detailed controls and checks imposed from outside the teaching institution. As they state:

> Dedication to high standards of performance is more easily promoted through shared professional norms than by bureaucratic sanctions and controls. (p34)

> Both quality and control in the school organization are enhanced when motivation and standards are internalized, because the most powerful accountability mechanisms come from professional norms and standards. (p41)

At this point a caveat needs to be sounded. It is probably true to say that the old adage in English education that 'teacher knows best', in the past applied to parents as much as to their children, is generally seen today as being coloured with more than a tinge of arrogance. A question must be faced: how does the professional group safeguard its standards and the trust it seeks and expects from the community which employs its members in the case of the maverick or incompetent professional? Of all the professional groupings in education - primary, secondary, further (or tertiary) and higher - the question may at first appear least relevant to the university sector, where observance of the principle of academic freedom has traditionally been seen as paramount. Interestingly, Bligh, writing principally with reference to higher education, comments on the problem. Arguing that the

> claim to possess special competence is itself not immune from doubt and critical inquiry (1982, p126)

he sees regular peer reviews of an academic's teaching and research as an appropriate protective mechanism. From the standpoint of the individual university teacher, any kind of personal review, whether initiated by one's academic peers or by an outside authority, might be viewed as a threat to academic freedom. Bligh's position - not unreasonable - is that, in the long run, academic freedom hinges on favourable public opinion, which in turn depends on vigilance and a sense of responsibility on the part of the academic community. Therefore academic freedom, a privilege which has to be earned, is rightly defended in terms of guarding against the deterioration of standards from within the institution as opposed to watching for threats from outside. Bligh's line - internal reviews by peers - has obvious merit in relation to comparatively large institutions like universities which, concerned with their international as well as national profile, are well placed to check internal rot. This cannot be said with an equal degree of confidence for many, small, schools, where professional deviance en masse could erupt quickly in circumstances of minimal external controls. In such cases arguing the virtues of a self-accountable professional environment and academic freedom could simply descend into fine-sounding but worthless trumpeting.

Accountability - communicating with or mistrusting the professionals?

To assert that an individual or institution should be accountable raises a number of questions (Wagner 1989, pp1-3). Are there degrees of accountability? If so, what factors determine a particular degree of accountability? By what criteria should teachers be called to account? And precisely who is entitled to hold teachers accountable? Immediately it becomes clear that the issue is not a simple one. What does float to the surface fairly readily, though, is the presumption that to talk about accountability implies some kind of entitlement (or right) and that the individual or institution called to account is placed under some kind of corresponding obligation or duty. The state (concerned with protecting the right of young people to receive a quality education and with the cultivation of useful and responsible citizens), local authority and school/college governors (as employers) can all be said to be entitled to hold teachers accountable. Such an entitlement is extendible to other groups, such as employers, who may release employees to attend college, and to parents, who pay fees directly, or indirectly through taxes, for the education their children receive. But, as Wagner aptly asks (p131), in what sense should entitlement be seen to apply? Would governors or parents be entitled to require a teacher to withdraw a controversial book from a literature course? Or would the proprietor of a business releasing employees to enable them to attend college be entitled to require that a teacher refrain from encouraging students to think critically about the economics of the free market? There seems little doubt that accountability encompasses an entitlement to *explanations* from teachers, but to enlarge that entitlement to the point of requiring teachers' *compliance* with governors', employers' or parents' wishes would be to undermine the benefits suggested by a professional environment of the kind already considered. Furthermore, there is the specific matter of how teachers, as professionals, can legitimately expect to be permitted to conduct themselves. Wagner argues the point thus:

> A parent has every right to ask about the reasons which underlie a diagnosis and treatment of his child's illness, but it is not generally presumed that he should dictate to the physician what that treatment should be ... (p134)

> ... whether or not teaching is a profession, goals in education must still be chosen and have a setting in which they can be effectively pursued. (p135)

The difficulties relating to accountability so far considered are seriously aggravated when it comes to the criteria which, in the nature of accountability mechanisms, elbow their way to the foreground. To return to the ideology given expression in the 1988 Education Reform Act, one intention, laudable enough in itself, underlying the introduction of open enrolment in schools was to shift power from the producers of education to the consumers (Maclure 1988, pp28-9). Accompanying this measure was a commitment, enshrined in both section 22 of the Act and the Parent's Charter, to the compulsory provision of information by schools, to enable parents to compare one school with another. In this way the education service would, in the government's view, become more accountable to those it is designed to serve. But there is an underlying problem, namely the validity and completeness of the criteria on which comparisons will be made. Education has moved from the traditional input (or investment) approach to quality, which emphasises such factors as teacher numbers, books and equipment, to one centred on outputs, measured by, for instance, examination results, student completion rates, entry into employment and cost-effective provision. The tendency now is to concentrate on the measurable and to downgrade, or even ignore, those areas of education which the new order cannot straightforwardly accommodate. In this the influence of business and industry, concerned with determinate products and services where output and performance are amenable to measurement, is apparent (Wagner 1989, pp24-5). But education, if it really is to be education, reaches into the vast territory of values, embracing such vital concerns as the individual's moral obligations, attitudes and wider questions of human purpose, where talk of quantification rapidly becomes plain nonsense. If mere evasion is the tack to be adopted, the corollary must be that a dehumanised, spiritually impoverished future with a consequent threat to democratic institutions is placed firmly on the agenda.

A startling consideration when one reflects on the application of new, quantifiable yardsticks to English education is that those same yardsticks have been revered in the American context in the early years of the twentieth century, only to be found grievously wanting. Callahan (1962) describes in the preface to his *Education and the cult of efficiency* how by 1910 the scale of operations in both business and education had produced large organisations. The incorporation of business ideas and techniques into educational institutions was, perhaps, to be expected, but the *extent* of the influence of business needed an explanation beyond the impact of high status activity (business) on a sector (education) traditionally enjoying less prestige. Callahan states in his preface:

> I had expected more professional autonomy ... I was surprised and then dismayed to learn how many decisions they [administrators] made or were forced to make, not on educational grounds, *but as a means of appeasing their critics in order to maintain their positions* ... [Italics added]

After the launch of the first Russian sputnik in 1957, the administrators' response, predictably, was that there should be an increased emphasis on science and mathematics in the school curriculum. The essential point to note is that this response was not based primarily on educational considerations and, as such, indicates a lack, at the time, of what Callahan refers to as 'educational statesmanship' or 'educational leadership'. In chapter 10 - 'An American tragedy in education' - he focuses on the nature of the problem:

> ...the essence of the tragedy was in adopting values and practices indiscriminately and applying them with little or no consideration of educational values or purposes ... Perhaps the tragedy was not inherent in the borrowing from business and industry but only in the application ... the record shows that the emphasis was not at all on 'producing the finest product' but on the 'lowest cost'. (p244)

The solution identified by Callahan involves the creation of structures of control conducive to the exercise of professional autonomy, so reducing the vulnerability of administrators. Moreover, professional autonomy, Callahan suggests, is necessarily associated with persons of calibre and so educated and skilled that the community will be prepared to trust them to act autonomously.

Conclusions

In the light of the radical re-shaping of education during the 1980s, together with attitudes associated with that re-shaping, the pursuit of a fully fledged professional setting for teachers may seem rather like the stuff of pipedreams. Barber's observation, in his searching study of the role of teacher unions, that

> the pre-1980s model consistently failed almost half of the school population (Barber 1992, p118)

would appear to add considerable weight, in the context of a democracy, to the case for greater accountability of teachers. Although Barber stresses the importance of governors' and parents' support (p115) and of a balance between the aspirations of teachers and those of the wider community (p126), it is significant that he also draws attention to the need for teachers to have

> considerable control over their work, and space in which to be creative. (p126)

The essential thread coursing through the present discussion is that, while it is perfectly proper for the community's representatives to call upon teachers to provide explanations and justifications for the manner in which they discharge their responsibilities, a clear distinction must be made between matters of explanation and justification on the one hand and intrusions into the professional domain on the other. It is appropriate to ask, of course, at precisely what point legitimate demands for accountability translate into intrusions, and, indeed, whether the notion of a dividing line can sensibly be sustained in the current environment of scarce resources and the need to achieve value for money. The conclusion implicit in the above examination of the issues and evidence is that such a dividing line does exist and that to allow erosion of the conditions necessary for an inclusive professional culture to prosper - which means insisting on a high standard of education (not merely 'competence') and a professionally autonomous environment for all teachers - will not merely demoralise and debilitate the teaching force, but will in effect undermine government's own search for a highly skilled, productive workforce.

This general position stated, it is accepted, as indicated earlier, that there will be those rare instances when an institution as a whole, either through collective arrogance or untempered commitment to dogma on the part of some or all of the staff, diverts to a course which both professionals outside and the wider community rate as irrational and injurious. From the professional perspective, it is perhaps to be regretted that in England (unlike Scotland) no General Teaching Council (consisting of both teachers and laypersons) yet exists which, functioning on lines comparable to the General Medical Council, could intervene decisively in cases of institutional breakdown such as the William

Tyndale School affair (Tomlinson, J. 1993, pp122-3). However, whatever machinery is set in place to deal with unacceptable deviations from stipulated norms, there needs to be a bedrock of communication, understanding and, perhaps above all, of trust between teachers and those to whom they are accountable. In this connection Wagner (1989, pp137-8) speaks, constructively, of 'accountability relationships' involving a 'rationally focused' approach to authority structures. This, Wagner explains, should be a two-way process, thus extending the idea of collegiality beyond professional groupings into the communities they serve. The outcome to be extrapolated from Wagner's thinking - bearing in mind the totality of the democratic process, including equipping young people for life in a democracy - is that society must guarantee teachers scope to pursue their tasks in an environment conducive to the exercise of responsible professional discretion. This means *encouraging* (not merely tolerating) a critical as well as a creative attitude in teachers vis-à-vis those responsible for controlling and resourcing educational institutions. Teachers, for their part, must acknowledge, unequivocally, a duty to society, firstly, to be open and clear about what they are doing and why they are doing it and, secondly, to address conscientiously and in an informed way educational issues and the effectiveness of their contribution as professionals.

A final note - must our future be our past?

This discussion began with a brief mention of an apparently erroneous assumption entrenched in the pre-1989 regimes of eastern Europe. Today many people whose fate was to be born and live under those regimes are grappling with the devastation and decay which has become their bitter legacy. Perhaps the future prosperity of their nations depends in part at least in never allowing their tragedy to be forgotten. As for the far-reaching changes which have impressed themselves on English education in the 1980s, there is a temptation to assume that the lessons of Callahan's American tragedy have been allowed to sink too far into the past for us to be able to confront seriously the possibility that future generations will inherit a legacy they will spurn and despise. But any temptation to make assumptions begins to fuse into alarm when it is recalled that, here in England, we have had our own more distant tragedy - the system of payment by results which, as Barnard describes (1961, pp113-14) made a mockery of education besides demoralising, degrading and corrupting teachers. If we are genuine in our efforts to come to grips with current and future concerns, we would do well to take careful note of our past.

References

Armytage, W.H.G. (1964), *Four hundred years of English education.* London: Cambridge University Press.

Barber, M. (1992), *Education and the teacher unions.* London: Cassell.

Barnard, H.C. (1961), *A history of English education from 1760* (second edition). London: University of London Press.

Beckett, F. (1993), *A 'vision for the future' but you're not part of it.* Guardian Education: 2 March 1993.

Birley, D. (1970), *The education officer and his world.* London: Routledge and Kegan Paul.

Bligh, D., (1982), *Freedoms, rights and accountability* in Bligh, D. (ed), *Accountability or freedom for teachers?* Guildford, Surrey: The Society for Research into Higher Education.

Callahan, R.E. (1962), *Education and the cult of efficiency.* Chicago: The University of Chicago Press.

Capitanchik, D. (1994) in University Life; Vol 1, No 2.

Coffield, F. (1990), *From the decade of the enterprise culture to the decade of the TECs* in Esland, G. (1991), *Education, training and employment* (Vol 2). Wokingham: Addison-Wesley Publishing Company/The Open University.

Department of Education and Science (DES) (1985), *Education and training for young people* (Cmnd 9482). London: HMSO.

DES (1991), *The parent's charter* (revised edition: October 1991). London: DES.

DES etc (May 1991), *Education and training for the 21st century* (Cm 1536). London: HMSO.

Devaney, K. and Sykes, G. (1988), *Making the case for professionalism* in Lieberman, A. (ed), *Building a professional culture in schools.* New York: Teachers College Press, Columbia University.

Employment Department (1990), *1990s: the skills decade: strategic guidance on training and enterprise.* Sheffield: Employment Department.

Fowler, G. (1977), *Curriculum control; a review of the issues* in Glatter, R. (ed), *Control of the curriculum: issues and trends in Britain and Europe* (Proceedings of the Fifth Annual Conference of the British Educational Administration Society. London: September 1976. (Studies in Education (new series) 4). London: University of London Institute of Education.

Further Education Funding Council (England) (FEFC(E)) (1992), *Funding learning.* London: FEFC(E).

Hymas, C. (1993), *Comprehensive to set own teachers' salaries.* The Sunday Times: 30 May 1993.

Institute for Public Policy Research (1993), *Education: a different vision (an alternative white paper)*. London: Institute for Public Policy Research.

Jackson, M. (1991), *Free market route to ruin*. The Times Educational Supplement (TES): 7 June 1991.

Jonathan, R. (1987), *The Youth Training Scheme and core skills: an educational analysis* in Holt, M. *Skills and vocationalism: the easy answer*. Milton Keynes: Open University Press.

Knight, B. (1993), *Beyond the budget*. TES: 11 June 1993.

Lawton, D. (ed) (1989), *The Education Reform Act: choice and control* London: Hodder and Stoughton.

Maclure, S. (1988), *Education re-formed*. Sevenoaks, Kent: Hodder and Stoughton.

McGinty, J. and Fish, J. (1993), *Further education in the market place*. London: Routledge.

Maxwell, E. (1994), *Four into one means one for all*. TES: 6 May 1994.

McLaughlin, M.W. and Yee, S.M-L. (1988), *School as a place to have a career* in Lieberman, A. (ed), *Building a professional culture in schools*. New York: Teachers College Press, Columbia University.

Merrick, N. (1994), *FE claims an unfair contest*. TES: 13 May 1994.

Murray, R. (1991), *Fordism and post-Fordism* in Esland, G. (ed), *Education, training and employment*, Vol 1. Wokingham: Addison-Wesley Publishing Company/The Open University.

Salter, B. and Tapper, T. (1981), *Education, politics and the state*. London: Grant McIntyre.

Tomlinson, J. (1993), *The control of education*. London: Cassell.

Tomlinson, P. and Kilner, S. (undated), *The flexible approach to learning: a guide*. Employment Department.

Wagner, R.B. (1989), *Accountability in education*. London: Routledge.

Williams, G. (1980), *Resources for FE/HE in the 1980s*. Bristol: Further Education Staff College (Coombe Lodge Report: Vol 13; No 11).

8 The concept of competence in primary teaching

Mary Jane Drummond

Abstract

This paper takes as its point of departure the reflective diary written by an experienced infant teacher in an attempt to come to terms with the difficult behaviour of one of her pupils. From arguing that the technical 'competence' already possessed in full measure by this teacher takes little account of what is required by the situation, the paper moves to examining the concept of competence more generally; concluding, with reference to Fromm, Simone Weil and other philosophers of existence, that human dimensions of teaching, like the sense of self that teachers bring to their work, and the attentive engagement of teachers with children's minds, escape the net of 'competence' as this is typically manifested in tick-lists and would-be exhaustive sets of skills and criteria.

Introduction

On 8 September 1993, Thomas started school. He was nearly five years old, and at first attended half-time only, building up towards full-time attendance by the October half-term. His teacher was Janice Brown, an experienced infant teacher and deputy head of a first school. Within days Thomas had made his mark on the even tenor of classroom life, apparently indifferent to his teacher's benevolent aspirations for a quiet and orderly community of reception class children. Janice Brown recorded her early impressions in diary form:

Thomas' fifth session was a Tuesday afternoon and he arrived in a very lively state; he ran shrieking extremely loudly across the room and then came back to where I was standing with his Mother. I quietly tried to explain again about the way we enter a room, at which he ran and shrieked all the way across the room and back. He ran full force into me and thumped my stomach with his hands. Before I could say or do anything Thomas' Mother said 'He is so very excited about coming to school, he looks forward to it so much. He cannot understand why he doesn't come to school all day. I was wondering when he will be having an increase in sessions.' I felt like saying 'NEVER!' but I refrained.

In the weeks that followed, Janice Brown continued to make regular detailed observations of what she saw as Thomas' disruptive behaviour:

In the early part of the term, if I asked him to sit down and join the others, he would refuse or go and sit somewhere else. If I asked him to do something quietly he would do it making a noise. If I asked him to walk, he would run, and if I asked him to run, he would walk. Thomas seemed to derive great pleasure in doing the opposite of whatever was suggested. He would laugh, smirk, smile; he would dance around singing loudly or even hold his hands in a 'claw position' and would hiss and snarl at myself or the other adults in the room. He would also be provocative in his spoken and body language.

At the end of September Janice Brown started a sixty hour course at the Cambridge Institute of Education. This course, *Early Years Care and Education,* of which I was the tutor, is part of our modular programme for the Advanced Diploma in Educational Studies; for her written assignment, part of the formally assessed work for the Diploma, Janice decided to study Thomas even more intently. At our first supervision session, she asked herself a stream of questions about Thomas and her response to him - questions that urgently needed attention. She returned to her classroom the next day ready to embark on the task of trying to answer them.

Over the next two terms, Janice continued observing, analysing, reflecting; she completed her written work in April 1994. In supervising and then reading the completed assignment, which she entitled '*What are you doing, Thomas?*', I was being given an insider's view of Janice's learning as she pieced together a fuller and stronger understanding of what was going on. These experiences helped me to understand how very little room there is for the concept of competence in the work of primary teaching, or in the lives of primary teachers. Janice is both experienced and competent; and she did not know what to do. She is not incompetent; and she was at a loss.

In this paper I will hold the concept of competence up against what I know of primary teaching, and outline some of its inadequacies, its omissions and distortions. In particular I will consider how an approach to effective teaching based on competencies does not take account of the crucial sense of self that teachers bring to their work; how it ignores the importance of teachers' learning, and teachers' moral powers; how in emphasising skill, technique and strategy, it neglects teachers' questions, and their attentive engagement with children's minds. Elliot Eisner's fine words 'Our nets define what we shall catch' (quoted in Whitehead 1992) suggest that even as the competence approach draws in a shoal of competent teachers, other more effective and more fully human teachers may be lost to primary education.

The concept of competence has a written history; other authors in this volume have described its birth, childhood and maturity. More important for practising teachers is its application to their lives in schools. I was introduced to some of these practical applications when moderating PGCE (primary) students on their final school experiences (at two other universities) in the summer of 1992. Before starting the school visits to observe students in action, I had already been alarmed by the detailed criteria for assessment, printed in the course handbook for one PGCE course, which, for all their detail, seemed to me to omit so much. I had searched the small print in vain for attention to children's spontaneity and imagination, for a sense of open-endedness or creativity, for an awareness of the emotional lives of children. I found, instead, an emphasis on objectives, activities, materials and tasks. Criteria for assessing classroom management included communication techniques, the use of the voice and the ability to manage children; the list of desirable outcomes did not refer to choice, freedom, independence or autonomy.

These criteria, though clearly inadequate as a description of primary teaching as I understand it, did not prepare me for the completed tick sheets I was given as I started my visits to schools. These sheets were being used by university tutors and school staff members as part of the assessment process.

Figure 1

	School's Comments		Tutor's Comment	
Preparation and planning	Good		Good	
	Satisfactory		Satisfactory	
	Needs Attention		Needs Attention	
	Cause for Concern		Cause for Concern	

Figure 1 continued../..

Classroom management	Good	☐	Good	☐
	Satisfactory	☐	Satisfactory	☐
	Needs Attention	☐	Needs Attention	☐
	Cause for Concern	☐	Cause for Concern	☐

Relationship with pupils	Good	☐	Good	☐
	Satisfactory	☐	Satisfactory	☐
	Needs Attention	☐	Needs Attention	☐
	Cause for Concern	☐	Cause for Concern	☐

Use of resources	Good	☐	Good	☐
	Satisfactory	☐	Satisfactory	☐
	Needs Attention	☐	Needs Attention	☐
	Cause for Concern	☐	Cause for Concern	☐

Assessment and and record keeping	Good	☐	Good	☐
	Satisfactory	☐	Satisfactory	☐
	Needs Attention	☐	Needs Attention	☐
	Cause for Concern	☐	Cause for Concern	☐

Self evaluation	Good	☐	Good	☐
	Satisfactory	☐	Satisfactory	☐
	Needs Attention	☐	Needs Attention	☐
	Cause for Concern	☐	Cause for Concern	☐

Role in school	Good	☐	Good	☐
	Satisfactory	☐	Satisfactory	☐
	Needs Attention	☐	Needs Attention	☐
	Cause for Concern	☐	Cause for Concern	☐

Teaching of subject specialism	Good	☐	Good	☐
	Satisfactory	☐	Satisfactory	☐
	Needs Attention	☐	Needs Attention	☐
	Cause for Concern	☐	Cause for Concern	☐

Cause for concern	Yes	No	Yes	No
In danger of failing	Yes	No	Yes	No

Any other comment:

This schedule was completed roughly halfway through the final school experience, and formed part of the half-term review, at which students would be informed if, in any way, they were giving cause for concern. Discussions with groups of successful students later that week added to my first alarms: the students were well aware of the ineffectiveness of this approach. They saw this system as relying heavily on a deficit model of their teaching, documenting what each of them was doing least well or failing to do at all. The students confirmed my suspicions that the format was not being used (and indeed could not be used) to identify their growing points or promising areas of development. In Vygotskian terms, the ticksheet did not encourage the supervising tutor or the host teacher to nurture the buds or blossoms of the students' learning. These sixty-four little boxes could not be used to identify a student's 'zone of proximal development'.

Figure 2

1 / Direct Instruction	2 / Guided Practice	3 / Structured
4 / Management of	5 / Monitoring and	Conversation
Materials	Assessment	6 / Management of Order
7 / Planning	8 / Evaluation	9 / Ethos

Please tick levels demonstrated

Dimension	Level 1	Level 2	Level 3
1			
2			
3			
4			
5			
6			
7			
8			
9			

Phase 2 and Phase 3 only please indicate

Pass/Fail

At another university I encountered a similar system - nine dimensions of teaching, each to be assessed at Levels one to three (see above).

Detailed criteria were provided for students, teachers, supervising tutors and external examiners. Nevertheless, these twenty-seven boxes cannot possibly be an adequate map of the challenges of classroom life. And there are patent absurdities built into this particular model. Consider the 'ethos' dimensions: if experienced teachers such as myself (or my readers, or co-authors) were to look back over their classroom years as an exercise in retrospective grading, how many rainy Friday afternoons would come out at Level 3?

This whole apparatus, criteria, boxes, ticks and all, has been drawn up by serious, committed,well-intentioned teacher educators, in the interests, presumably, of precision, comparability and reliability. But the physical scientist's devotion to accuracy and exactitude is here misapplied. As Rolph Schwarzenberger (1987) so drily comments in a challenging paper on pupils' learning: 'the more accurately an attainment can be measured, the less likely is it to reflect genuine understanding'. (p6)

The examples I have given above illustrate a desire for precision and a search for detached objectivity that are, in my view, unhelpful in trying to understand or evaluate what teachers do in classrooms. The competence approach too is driven by such a desire and such a search; it is similarly inappropriate as a tool for examining teaching. Not only does the competence approach assume fixity and objectivity where I see unpredictability, provisionality and subjectivity, it also ignores almost everything that I believe to be important in the tasks that teachers daily set themselves in their classrooms.

The competence approach omits, first, any account of the teacher's sense of self - that sense of individual and personal aspiration for the effectiveness of one's teaching that all teachers bring to bear, every day, on the thousands of unpredictable incidents that make up classroom life. Jennifer Nias (1989) has documented the personal and professional experiences of primary teachers in vivid biographical detail. Drawing on extensive interview data with ninety-nine primary teachers, Nias gives 'an insider's account of teaching'. She concludes: 'the most pervasive and persistent theme to emerge from this study is the centrality to individual teachers of their sense of self'. She argues that in interpreting this theme we must accept that 'teaching as work requires its practitioners to be self-conscious' (p202). That is, we must accept that the self is a crucial element in the way teachers themselves construe the nature of their job.

Erich Fromm, psycho-analyst and sociologist, approaches the same theme in a different way. The aim of life, he writes in *The Sane Society* (1956), 'is to live it intensely, to be fully born, to be fully awake, to be convinced of one's real but limited strength'. He describes the crippling anxiety caused by the lack of this conviction, by the lack of self: 'Inasmuch as 'I am as you desire me' - *I* am *not*; I am anxious, dependent on others, constantly trying to please' (p204). Teachers who strive to be, in Fromm's sense, as others desire them, are 'not' - not people, not teachers, but, he goes on to suggest, robots, who have resigned the use of their powers and talents, their ability 'to love, to think, to laugh, to cry, to wonder and to create' (p205). Here Fromm is developing a despairing theme he first discussed in *Fear of Freedom* (1942), where he roundly castigates 'modern man' for his failings, and for adopting a self which is not his. 'The more he does this, the more powerless he feels, the more he is forced to conform' (p220). In this condition, 'one can be sure of oneself only if one lives up to the expectations of others'. The result is a profound doubt of one's own identity. 'If I am nothing but what I believe I am supposed to be - who am 'I'?' (p219). The only antidote is the spontaneous activity of the total personality, where spontaneity is defined as the free activity of the self, the use of the creative will, in which 'the individual embraces the world' (p225).

The origins of these human ills are to be found, according to Fromm, not in ourselves, but in the society we have shaped for ourselves. In a long chapter called *Man in Capitalist Society* (Fromm 1956) he imagines what would happen if things could speak and we were to interrogate them ... Who are you? He lists the imaginary answers of things and people, and muses over their similarities.

I am a typewriter
I am a Cadillac
I am a manufacturer
I am a clerk
I am the father of two kids (p142)

Man, 'the only animal that can say I', has ceased to see himself as a person with powers, talents, strengths, as a man with love, fear, convictions, doubts; he sees himself as an abstraction 'which fulfils a certain function in the social system'. The teacher who is seen as a fully ticked-off list of competencies would be just such a functional abstraction, an impoverished 'thing'.

The competence model of what it is to be a teacher omits another huge area of experience: teachers' learning, especially the emotional dimension of that learning, which I have discussed more fully elsewhere

(Drummond and McLaughlin 1994). The teacher shaped by pre-determined competencies may indeed be incapacitated for learning. In a striking analysis of the concept of self-esteem in the context of teaching and learning, the psychologist Guy Claxton (1990) identifies some current myths about high self-esteem (before exploding them, with a satisfying finality).

1   Worthwhile people do not make mistakes. Worth is contingent on competence. Incompetence is unworthy and must be paid for with guilt, shame or loss of self-esteem.

2   Worthwhile people always know what is going on. Worth is contingent on clarity. Confusion and feeling out of control are unworthy and should be paid for with a loss of self-esteem.

3   Worthwhile people live up to, and within, their images of themselves. Worth is contingent on consistency. Acting unpredictably, out of character or in defiance of one's precedents and principles is unworthy and must be paid for with a loss of self-esteem.

4   Worthwhile people do not feel anxious, apprehensive, fraught or fragile. Worth is contingent on feeling cool, calm and collected. Feeling nervous, overwhelmed or ill-tempered should be paid for with a loss of self-esteem. (p137)

These myths, Claxton shows, are dangerous. Competent, clear, consistent, cool teachers are not likely to be effective learners; they will experience learning, according to him, as an assault on their established and cherished pictures of themselves (clear, cool and competent). Claxton suggests that these people will be threatened by learning, with its new insights, new opportunities, new challenges; their rational response to it will be defence. Competent people, whose prime purpose is to remain competent, will work hard to preserve and maintain what they already know, or can do, or are.

Here Claxton is echoing, perhaps unconsciously, a fundamental dichotomy in human possibilities, eloquently described by Matthew Arnold in 1869, in *Culture and Anarchy*. Arnold contrasts 'a having and a resting' with 'a growing and a becoming', developing two opposing, polarised (and inevitably, exaggerated) styles of living one's life. In one, we are possessed with a determination to get things done; there is a paramount sense of the obligation of duty, self-control and work. In the other, there is a commitment, not to action, but to thinking things out, driven by 'the indomitable impulse to know and adjust'. In one, the uppermost idea is right conduct and obedience; in the other, it is to see things as they really are. Strictness of conscience, in the one, is replaced in the other by the spontaneity of consciousness (chapter IV op cit). And spontaneity, as we have seen, has no place in a model of teaching predicated on competence. Arnold's vision of human excellence, and his definition of culture as the study of human perfection, are worlds away from the competence approach.

More recent critics of the concept of competence have identified another absence for comment and concern. David Carr (1993) has more than one argument for banishing 'an improper idea of competencies' for its crime of 'serious violence to any coherent conception of rational and principled educational practice' (p255). Here I will only refer to his discussion of the moral basis of what teachers do. Carr argues convincingly that 'deciding what is best for children is at heart a moral and evaluative matter'. Serious educational debate cannot be carried out in the absence of 'rational moral reflection'. Serious teachers are characterised by their 'real moral commitment' to the goals that they have strenuously debated and defined for themselves. Of course, Carr is not the only philosopher of education with an interest in the moral domain; in a recent lecture at the Cambridge Institute (1991, unpublished) Mary Warnock insisted, again and again, on the inescapable moral dimension of teachers' lives. 'Education must convey moral messages ... Teaching is a job with a moral commitment from morning to night ... The school is set up to convey moral messages ...' The lecture was memorable however, not for these particular messages, but for the first question from the floor; a teacher urgently asked about the propriety of 'imposing values' on her pupils. The question was summarily dismissed ('If you don't go in to impose values, you may as well give up teaching'), but the fact that it was asked at all does perhaps indicate that, as a professional group, teachers are not as clear as they might be about their moral responsibilities, about their powers to make moral decisions in the interests of children. The competence model will not help them to understand more clearly.

David Carr, too, is concerned about values, and how they inform teaching. He argues that descriptions of competencies, the things that teachers are required to do, have become disconnected from the explicit value positions from which they were originally defined, and so their usefulness is severely limited. He contrasts different kinds of failure: failure of skill or technique, failure of moral attitude or value, failure of understanding. The competence model can only identify or accommodate the first of these; 'the bare causal efficacy' of what the teacher does is not an adequate basis for judging the teacher's necessary moral understanding of teaching and learning (Carr op cit, p270).

While those who work with the competence model prescribe skills and techniques, and identify the observable behaviours that would constitute convincing evidence of any particular competence, I am in good company in calling for any account of educational practice to do more, much more. Both Hyland (1993) and Norris (1991) give searching accounts of the model's inadequacies; to their list I would add the lack of reference to the teacher's attention to children's thinking, or to the teacher's engagement with children's minds. Essentially unobservable, this engagement would be, in pedagogy of quality, whole-hearted but provisional in form, respectful, informed by children's learning in the recent past, and enlarged by the prospect of learning in the future. (Incidentally, Fromm reminds us in passing that the virtue of respect, which he regards most highly, has its etymological roots in the Latin *respicere*: to look again, to see things and people as they really are.)

The teacher's engagement with children's thinking will, at its most effective, be deeply attentive, in the sense in which Simone Weil uses the term. For Weil, the word 'attention' conveys the act of putting oneself in someone else's place, listening for justice and virtue, being alive to truth and to affliction: 'The spirit of justice and truth is nothing else but a certain kind of attention' (Weil 1986, p91). At one and the same time, furthermore, the attentive teacher will be one step behind the child, embodying the Froebelian ideal of 'the following teacher' (Liebschner 1992), and one step ahead, ready to participate in the task that, following Vygotsky (1978), we have come to think of as scaffolding and supporting the child's presently developing learning.

This chapter began at the beginning of the school year, with the first encounter between a child and his teacher. As the term continued, Janice Brown's attention to Thomas did not waver. Though sometimes anxious, sometimes provoked, sometimes impatient, she continued to watch, to listen and to ask herself questions. Her own account of what she saw and what she did during this time reminded me of Iris Murdoch's account of 'attention' as the work of the active moral agent. 'Clear vision,' claims Murdoch, 'is a result of moral imagination and moral effort' (1985, p37). She reaches this conclusion by analysing an imaginary example: 'a mother, whom I shall call M, feels hostility to her daughter-in-law, whom I shall call D'. With the passage of time, M changes her mind; her vision of D alters. Murdoch describes M's thinking as essentially progressive, as infinitely perfectible, but combined with a built-in notion of necessary fallibility: 'M is engaged in an endless task'. This is because she is trying 'not just to see D accurately, but to see her justly or lovingly' (p23).

For Janice Brown, the beginning of clearer vision, of a more loving understanding, came in mid-October.

October 21, pm. We played a *Look and Read* card game. Thomas joined in well. Later, when it was time to tidy up, Thomas began to throw the cards around. I said to him three times 'Don't throw the cards, please, Thomas, they will get damaged. If you damage the cards, we won't be able to play the game again.' The other children in the group also protested and tried to stop him. Eventually I said, 'if you throw the cards again, I will be very cross'.

Far from complying, Thomas laughed, and threw the cards in his teacher's face, asking 'How cross?'. The teacher was, in her own words, furious.

I shouted 'Very cross!' Everything went silent in the room. I had never shouted at any of the children before. Thomas looked shocked. The other children quickly picked up the cards with Thomas and put them in my lap.

Looking back, she wrote 'how dare this four year old question my authority?' But when she next arrived at the Institute for her Diploma course, she was eager to talk about what had happened, fascinated by the way in which Thomas' behaviour seemed to have changed following the incident.

We broke up for half term holiday the same afternoon and my next observation of Thomas was not until Monday, November 1, 1993, the first day back after the holidays.

There was quite a change in Thomas that day. He worked well, concentrated, played co-operatively with another child and tidied up when it was time to do so.

Janice Brown explained how after she had shouted at Thomas, she had felt deflated, guilty, manipulated, dissatisfied with herself. And yet, in a sense, she felt she had answered Thomas' question ('How cross?') with a new honesty. In the past she had responded to Thomas' attempts to explore the boundaries of acceptable and unacceptable behaviour with professional self-restraint. While he was working, as it now seemed to her, with all his might, to find out how to enrage and infuriate her with transgressions of classroom routines, she had responded with the (almost) endless patience of the experienced reception class teacher. Her ability to keep calm, her refusal to get 'Very cross' had continually frustrated Thomas' attempts to understand how she worked and how she compared with the other adults he knew best. She realised, as she reflected on the incident, that for the first time since they met, she had been able to see an acceptable purpose in Thomas' deviant behaviour. Seeing Thomas, not just more accurately, but more justly and lovingly, in Murdoch's phrase, entailed re-defining his non-compliance as systematic enquiry. Thomas did not share his teacher's interest in classroom rules and routines; his interest was in more volatile and immediate areas of experience - his personal relationships with adults and children. As a result of this internal act of re-definition, Janice Brown's own relationship with Thomas was radically changed. Her written account ends with the optimistic words: 'Thomas is an interesting individual. He has stimulated my thoughts on a variety of issues. I hope I can do likewise!'

Janice Brown had not, it goes without saying, added a new competence to her professional repertoire. Nor had she moved from Level 2 to Level 3 in the Management of Order dimension (shown in Figure 2). The official list of requirements for the newly qualified secondary teacher, as laid down in circular 9/92 (DFE 1992) has, likewise, nothing to say about teachers like Janice Brown. It is impossible to do justice to her significant learning, which she had undertaken at the cost of considerable pain, with such arid frameworks as these.

It is then thoroughly alarming that there is no shortage of further material, from thoroughly official sources, advocating a view of effective teaching in terms of what is procedurally appropriate at a technical level (Carr 1994). Take, for example, the report by HMI *Aspects of Primary Education in France* (DES 1991). Here we read of competent and confident teachers.

> They used exposition and questioning effectively to teach the whole class the same things at the same time and their blackboard work was exemplary (paragraph 67).

These paragons even pay attention to learning:

> In all the lessons, the teacher continually checked that learning was taking place by asking questions and checking the work on the slates or exercise books (paragraph 18).

It is as easy as that. In another report, *Well-managed classes in primary schools: case studies of six teachers* (OFSTED 1993), there are descriptions of a number of lessons given by six 'effective but not exceptional teachers', whose names have been changed. One of these is Mrs Cadman, who teaches Year 1; her class of twenty-eight children was observed in a dance lesson. Mrs Cadman's teaching is notated in detail. for example:

> She uses a tambourine to good effect to accompany the children's movement and to demonstrate how the movement begins at the finger-tips and works its way through the body ... At this stage she introduces a refinement in that the pupils can only begin their sequences once the tambourine has passed over their heads.

The OFSTED inspectors may call this a refinement if they choose; I prefer to cling to other ways of seeing, in which we may recognise Mrs Cadman's techniques for what they are - a benevolent but despotic use of adult power and authority, which requires obedience from the dependent and silent pupils. It is some relief to find that the lesson ends with the time-honoured ritual of 'dead fishes', suitably disguised for the Inspectors, I presume, since they describe it as a 'good example of her skillful management of the class'.

When Mrs Cadman lies in bed at night, does she, I wonder, ask herself questions, about her teaching, about her children's learning? Do the French teachers, away from their blackboards, wonder about the quality of their pupils' learning? Or about the ideas in their heads that never get transferred onto their slates? Might not the quality of teachers' questions about their effectiveness be as important as the polish of their techniques?

My own experience of in-service work with a wide variety of teachers and other educators over the last ten years has convinced me that the ability and resolution to ask piercing questions about normally taken-for-granted classroom events are absolutely essential ingredients of effectiveness. Teachers who have stopped asking questions have reached, pedagogically, the end of the road. There is nothing more for them to do, nowhere else for them to go. They cannot aspire to Stenhouse's vision (1985) of the teacher as research scientist crossed with creative artist. Through self-monitoring, Stenhouse argues, (and we may take self-monitoring to be a form of self-questioning)

> the teacher becomes a conscious artist. Through conscious art, he is able to use himself as an instrument of his research (p16)

Janice Brown did not make such claims for herself explicit; but she knew she was researching the heart of her own practice, and she trusted the power of her questions to shed light on what she wanted to know. The last page of her written assignment is studded with further questions; not 'what' and 'how' questions about skills and techniques, but 'why' questions that reach to the moral core of her life as a teacher. There is no place in the competence model for the questions that Janice Brown has committed herself to go on asking, not just about Thomas, but about everything she does in the name of teaching and learning. Norris' powerful critique of the competence approach (1991) concludes that we do not need to set ourselves standards of pedagogical performance (which, in any case, cannot be adequately specified). Instead we need standards of criticism and principles of judgement (p337). To these requirements I would add one more: we also need the continuous exercise of purposeful enquiry.

In enquiring into and learning about our teaching, we will also, I believe, learn about ourselves: all to the good. Tolstoy's experiment in primary education did not last long enough to ensure his enduring popularity as a prophet of progressivism, but his accounts of the school he set up on his estate at Yasnaya Polyana do make fascinating and rewarding reading. In particular, they show how clearly he understood the centrality of teachers' learning in the effective education of their children.

> Education presents itself as a complex and difficult matter, only so long as we wish, without educating ourselves, to educate our children or any one else. But if we come to understand that we can educate others only through ourselves, the question of education is made void, and only the question of life is left, 'How must I live myself?' I do not know a single act in the education of children which is not included in the education of oneself. (McAllister 1931, p399)

Writing of his pupils, Tolstoy uses a striking metaphor, which will serve as an end-piece to this paper. At times, he writes, the children's attention and diligence were so evident that he feared they would 'submit to the cunning of the nets of order and so lose the possibility of choice and protest' (McAllister op cit, p391). We may extend this metaphor and this insight to primary teachers today; if we urge them to submit to the cunning of the nets of competence, they will lose other more educationally valuable possibilities. Above all they will lose the possibility of choosing to give children (their fine minds, their growing understanding) the attention they deserve in the most fully human way. In Simone Weil's words: 'The name of this intense, pure, disinterested, gratuitous, generous attention is love.' (Weil 1986, p91)

References

Arnold, M. (1869), *Culture and Anarchy*, 1932 edition. Cambridge: Cambridge University Press.

Carr, D. (1993), Questions of Competence *British Journal of*

Educational Studies 41 (3), 253-271.

Carr, D. (1994), Wise Men and Clever Tricks *Cambridge Journal of Education* 24 (1), 89-106.

Claxton, G. (1990), *Teaching to Learn: a Direction for Education.* London: Cassell.

Department for Education (1992), *Circular 9/92: Initial Teacher Training (Secondary Phase).* London: DFE.

Department of Education and Science (1991), *Aspects of Primary Education in France: a Report by HMI.* London: DES.

Drummond, M.J. and McLaughlin, C. (1994), Teaching and Learning: the fourth dimension in Bradley, H., Conner, C. and Southworth, G. (eds), *Developing Teachers Developing Schools.* London: David Fulton.

Fromm, E. (1942), *The Fear of Freedom.* London: Routledge and Kegan Paul.

Fromm, E. (1956), *The Sane Society* (page references to 1991 enlarged edition). London: Routledge

Hyland, T. (1993), Competence, Knowledge and Education. *Journal of Philosophy of Education* 27 (1), 57-68.

Liebschner, J. (1992), *A Child's Work: Freedom and Play in Froebel's Educational Theory and Practice.* Cambridge: The Lutterworth Press.

McAllister, W.J. (1931), *The Growth of Freedom in Education.* London: Constable.

Murdoch, I. (1985), *The Sovereignty of Good.* London: Ark Paperbacks.

Nias, J. (1989), *Primary Teachers Talking: a study of teaching as work.* London: Routledge.

Norris, N. (1991), The Trouble with Competence. *Cambridge Journal of Education* 21 (3), 331-341.

Office for Standards in Education (1993), *Well-managed Classes in primary schools: case studies of six teachers.* London: DFE.

Schwarzenberger, R. (1987), *Targets for Mathematics in Primary Education.* Warwick Seminar on Public Education Policy Occasional Paper No 2. Trentham Books.

Stenhouse, L. (1985), *Research as a basis for teaching.* London: Heinemann.

Vygotsky, L.S. (1978), *Mind in society.* Cambridge, Mass.: Harvard University Press.

Weil, S. (1986), An Essay on Human Personality in Miles, S. (ed), *Simone Weil: an Anthology.* London: Virago.

Whitehead, M. (1992), Assessment at Key Stage 1: Teacher Assessment through record keeping in Blenkin, G. and Kelly, V. (eds), *Assessment in Early Childhood Education.* Paul Chapman Publishing.

Acknowledgement

I am very grateful to Janice Brown for allowing me to quote from her child-study, and for the many discussions we had together while she was writing it.

9 Tying up loose ends *or* blueprint for education for the next 25 years?

Peter McBride

Abstract

The Government hoped that the 1993 Education Act would lay the foundations for education for the next 25 years. It extended central control at the expense of LEAs in the name of choice and diversity. Its major ideological goal was to enhance the establishment of an internal market in which self-governing schools would play a primary role. To the Government's credit it did address many deficiencies in Special Needs provision, but the Act will be remembered more for its moral prescriptions intended to standardise and improve religious and sex education. In a continuing search for standards it changed attendance procedures and devised mechanisms for dealing with surplus places and failing schools. Interventionism was increased to obtain accountability, eradicate inefficiency and arrest a perceived fall in both moral and academic standards. The question remains, however: can central direction provide the consensus and flexibility necessary to correspond with constantly changing social and cultural values?

Introduction

For almost twenty years since 'The Great Debate', educational concerns have been focused on the following: accountability, value for money, standards and standardisation, parental choice and the balance of control between central, local and institutional government. The Green Paper 'Education in Schools' 1976 and the Taylor Report 'A New Partnership for our Schools' 1978 provide clear evidence that the major educational issues have remained relatively constant for almost two decades.

The legislative means of addressing these problems, however, reveal changing political values which have engendered structural shifts in both the balance of power and nature of relationships which now characterise our educational system. This short analysis of the 1993 Education Act is presented to illustrate these points.

It is also intended to provide some understanding of how concepts can be stretched to accord with political conventions to maintain an internal coherence, the price of which is necessarily the victory of one value system over another as opposed to any attempt to reach a consensual accord.

The 1993 Education Act consists of a great deal of 'unfinished business' following the Education Reform Act 1988, which itself was regarded as a watershed or a landmark to re-state and define the focus of power, responsibilities and relationships post-1944.

In the view of the Government there was still an ideological agenda to be pursued and completed. This was openly stated in the 1992 White Paper 'Choice and Diversity', which saw grant-maintained schools as the means of delivering its five main themes of: quality, diversity, increasing parental choice, greater autonomy for schools and greater accountability. The limitations of the 1981 Education Act, highlighted by the Audit Commission Report 1992 'Getting in on the Act'; the Department for Education consultation document, Special Educational Needs: Access to the System, illustrated a further aspect of unfinished business but perhaps of equal significance was the determination manifest in Part 1 to diminish, minimise, if not eliminate LEAs within the balance of the partnership.

Concern with attendance was in part a play to the law and order gallery. Attention given to 'failing' schools continues the search for means to achieve 'standards' which had escaped the legislative reach of governments since 1976. Coming so soon after the 1992 Schools Act, which had ostensibly dealt with inspection and monitoring, the feeling of revisiting old themes and tying up loose ends was much in evidence before the spate of miscellaneous sections were drawn together in Part 6. An Act of 300 sections seems long-winded, incoherent and petty, even contradictory, contrasted with the economic dramatic precision of its precursor 50 years earlier, ie, the Butler Act of 1944.

By further contrast, the 1944 Act took 18 months of consultation and negotiation before the Bill was presented to Parliament, whereas the 1993 Act was on the Statute Book exactly one year after the 1992 White Paper, which was the essence of what was to become the Bill and, in amended form, the 1993 Act.

Responsibility for education relocated from the locality to the centre

Part 1 of the Act is regarded by many, particularly the local authority associations, as the most significant feature of the Act. Section 7 of the 1944 Act had placed a burden on local education authorities (LEAs) to provide and ensure sufficient and appropriate primary, secondary and further education to meet the needs of their areas. The responsibility for further education was transferred by virtue of the Further and Higher Education Act 1992. Meanwhile, the creation of a Funding Agency for Schools which may combine with the LEA to plan for provision of grant-maintained (GM) schools or take over the function completely will, to say the least, reduce the role of the LEA.

This sharing of power was cited by the Association of Metropolitan Authorities (AMA), Association of County Councils (ACC), National Union of Teachers (NUT) and National Association of governors and Managers (NAGM), as creating a potentially different working relationship and as having a destabilising effect. Those opposed pointed to the loss of local democratic accountability, transfer of power from local to central government and the effective end of the partnership put in place by the 1944 Education Act. This seemed to be confirmed by Lady Blatch, Minister of State for Education, who emphasised the parallel and separate powers and duties of the Funding Agency and commented that LEAs would no longer have a pre-eminent role in the provision of education (Hansard 20.4.93). Thus quite clearly LEA monopoly of provision was to be ended.

Some saw the Funding Agency for Schools as comparable to Funding Councils for Further Education and the Funding Councils for Higher Education and undoubtedly the new body represents part of the continuing march towards centralisation. It is, however, noteworthy that the Agency will only apply the funding for the GM sector and will not determine the rules for funding like the Funding Councils. The Agency is more a pragmatic recognition that the supply of school places could not be left to the market entirely. The Agency indeed shares responsibility with the LEA for strategic planning where in either primary or secondary sectors 10% of pupils attend GM schools and takes total responsibility when that proportion exceeds 75%. The main role of the Funding Agency for Schools (FAS) is related to GM schools, which the Government expects or hopes will be the majority:

> to maintain them
> propose their creation
> make transitional arrangements
> alter instruments and articles of government.

The elected LEA and nominated FAS in this strange arrangement will be required solely or jointly to deal with an excess of places and in all events they are expected to liaise and work in harmony. If there were not sufficient evidence, Section 296, which repeals the requirement for LEAs to have education committees, confirms the intention to distance them from responsibilities placed on them in 1902. Ironically, the Education Act of that year was the culmination of a thirty year struggle to bring all forms of publicly provided or supported education under a single unified local authority.

The heart of the matter

The change put in place to favour predominantly self-governing institutions illustrates an ideological determination to focus provision at the institutional level, reinforce consumer sovereignty and provide competing cost centres to complete the internal market.

> At the Act's heart though is the Government's desire to increase the size of the Grant Maintained sector and further develop the managerial and financial structure. (Rogers 1993)

This was to be achieved in a number of ways. In the first instance, the Act now makes possible four alternative ways of creating GM schools, three of which are new:

> by ballot
> FAS creation
> proposal by any voluntary agency or private promoter
> joining a group of GM schools

To encourage the dynamic, the procedures for acquiring self-governing status have been streamlined by Sections 22-37 of the Act and thus:

- the requirement for Governors to pass a second resolution before proceeding to ballot on GM status is eliminated
- school government regulations require that a resolution on the ballot

issue be an agenda item notified to governors and other parties at least seven days prior to the meeting

- the overall time spent on the ballot process is shortened and action following a positive vote is speeded up
- impediments to transfer have been significantly removed so that it will be more difficult for hostile organisations to obstruct both pursuit and achievement of a 'successful outcome'. This is exemplified by the fact that the Secretary of State will reimburse governors for expenses involved in promotion of GM status, whilst LEA expenditure will be limited to the amount allocated to governing bodies. Restrictions on 'political' expenditure will continue to apply.

Ann Taylor, Labour's education spokesperson, claimed

> They do not want to talk about it, but selection is one of the objectives of the Bill. (19 March 1993 Education)

The 1988 Education Act had precluded a change in character for at least 5 years, later modified by allowing selection to facilitate specialisation. The Government had been sensitive about the issue but the new Act provides a wider opportunity, in so far as it enables a GM school to change in character or expand with relative ease. Because primary schools have so far been less attractive to move from local authority control, the Act allows groups of schools to opt out. This has been termed 'clustering small schools', which encourages the change by facilitating economies of scale or by domino effect within a given pyramid should one try to 'opt out'.

The linking of GM status with selectivity is reinforced when one notes that the Secretary of State may approve both change of character as well as increased admission limits in popular GM schools, whilst any comparable expansion by an LEA of its schools automatically allows a similar application by the GM school. The 85% grant available in voluntary aided schools may be added to by LEAs or FAS to encourage the transfer, whilst promoters of new GM schools can be helped with setting-up costs. One can hardly avoid the conclusion that the dice are being loaded to favour this particular kind of institution within the diversity of provision. Meanwhile LEAs may provide for the needs of GM schools by selling services for two years to enable the GM sector to buy in an independent established market sufficient to support self-governing schools.

In order to provide still further incentive to transition, a GM school may now be sponsored by an individual or company and the sponsor can propose up to four governors. Coincidentally, the Government have invented a £25 million scheme to fund specialisms in technology, mathematics and science available only in GM and aided schools. The sponsor need invest no more than £100,000 to attract the additional funding and the school can be regarded as a self-governing technology college. A cynic may be inclined to interpret this as recognition of the failure to attract the private sector to invest in City Technology Colleges to any significant extent. The Government's prior promotion of magnet special schools is undoubtedly a reflection of its belief in bringing business and education together in line with its policy on Compacts and one cannot disagree that this may attract more investment in education.

However, comments such as that of Conservative back bencher George Walden, who refers to comprehensive schools as,

a system of institutional mediocrity (19 March 1993 Education)

amplify the Prime Minister's reservations on the subject and thus create an impression that the Tory Government needs to resurrect Direct Grant Schools in a mutated form.

The range of innovations to create a diversity of schools which were variations on the self-governing theme has now created a confusing array of different types of Governors. The 'clustering' of schools introduces the concept of 'Core Governors'. We may now have 'Sponsoring Governors' to wed public and private sectors. 'Initial Governors' are necessary to initiate self-governing schools. Would-be creators of voluntary aided GM schools will be known as 'Promoting Governors', which adds to the long-standing 'Foundation Governors' in grant aided and voluntary schools. The complexity of institutions' governing regulations and relationships undoubtedly provides diversity but choice is hardly helped by confusion, and the difference of status implied by the new opportunities raises the question of whose choice and at whose expense?

Addressing the deficiencies

Government awareness of deficiencies in special needs provision can be seen in Chapter 9 of 'Choice and Diversity'. Indeed the Audit Commission Report 'Getting in on the Act' 1992 was the culmination of many earlier reports which revealed variable interpretations as well as means of implementing the 1981 Act.

The 1981 Act is based on the grand themes of the Warnock Report, which included a definition of the concept of special need in terms of:

additional response, the identification and statementing of children with special needs and teaching SEN children with others where possible. Such were the ideals which the 1981 Act attempted to address.

Some problems were evident from the original legislation in terms of loose terminology, vague specification of responsibilities and the obvious ramifications of assessment and statementing procedures. Perhaps, equally importantly, the Government legislated without recognising in any sense the financial implications of implementation. The net result was a lack of clarity surrounding the concept of special educational provision, diversity of practice among LEAs, lengthy assessment procedures and vagueness in statements.

Time taken for statementing varies between 10 months and 3 years. The number and percentage of statemented children in special schools has changed only marginally since 1982 and the percentage of children with statements varies from less than 1% to almost 3.5% between different LEAs. This led to the main conclusion of the Audit Commission 'Getting in on the Act' 1992, ie, that the key problems were lack of clarity with regard to definition and responsibilities, lack of accountability by both schools and LEAs for resources spent on special need, and, perhaps more importantly, no clear incentive or proper funding which would ensure implementation of the 1981 Act.

The extension of GM status to special educational needs schools hardly resolved any problems. The legislation did however bring in a new code of practice for schools and LEAs which would be developed subsequent to the 1993 Act. It increased parental powers to appeal with regard to statementing and created new Independent Tribunals to hear such appeals. Most significantly, it reinforced the role of the school in educating SEN children to ensure that integration is maximised and that practice is standardised.

The key to effective improvement as identified by the Audit Commission lies largely in the code of practice which lays down criteria for:

- moving to the statutory stages of assessment and statementing with time limits on the conduct of these stages
- clear and specific statements
- interaction and partnership between all involved with special need including LEA, parents and Health Authorities
- clear procedures for the involvement of children
- requirements to provide based on Warnock's three stages of response in school
- seeking advice from outside agencies or early identification and action.

The 1993 Act also restates duties of Governors with regard to SEN to ensure proper provision and to ensure all who need to know are informed. The requirement to publish a report on SEN within the annual report and specify the role of the SEN co-ordinator is further evidence that the legislation will have strong procedural regulations and this addresses one of the evident weaknesses in the 1981 Act. To many of the critics, the rights of parents are more fairly ensured to enable them to ask for review of special need provision whether or not a child has a statement. This is an attempt to break down the artificial and dangerous barrier erected by the concept of statementing, which distinguished effectively between 2% who had traditionally been educated separately and a further 18% all of whom Warnock estimated would fall into the SEN category within a school lifetime. The neglect of the 18% has always been the result of concentration on the 2% by LEAs.

The additional rights of parents reinforced by the Independent Tribunals would ensure that LEAs would abide by their statutory duty and apply their provision in the spirit of the Act and not in a manner affected by financial difficulties or arbitrary predilections to prioritise this aspect of education. What is more, the legislation attempts to give parents of special needs children a right to exercise choice about provision more akin to that of other parents. This must be consistent with the needs of the child and with the needs of those with whom s/he may be educated and again consistent with reasonable expenditure.

Responses to the changes are mixed. On the one hand, there is widespread approval of the new Code of Practice and Independent Tribunals; on the other, there is fear that increased rights of parents to veto irrespective of a child's needs may weaken the likelihood of integration. The Special Education Consortium summed it up:

> The question remains: will the changes made to the Government's original proposals prove sufficient protection to vulnerable children both with and without a statement in a market place where individual school autonomy is more highly prized than local responsibility? (Rogers, 1993)

In short, the Act does move further towards a rainbow of responses associated with the diversity of need but its success, like its predecessor in 1981, will depend on adequate resourcing. Although some loopholes have been closed, there remain ambiguities in determining a proper balance between the exercise of parental choice and provision of the child's need where possible within the mainstream.

Maintenance of standards

This is in part addressed by school attendance provisions. It is difficult to see a need for a major re-appraisal of school attendance procedures but the Act attempts to codify attendance requirements to educate children in accordance with age, ability and aptitude covered in Sections 36, 37 and 39 of the 1944 Act and largely confirmed in the 1980 Act. This is marginally complicated by education supervision orders which may be required under the Children Act 1989. However, a government committed to upholding standards, first raised as an issue by James Callaghan in his 1976 Ruskin speech, responds against a backcloth of increasing truancy which has been well publicised. At a practical level procedures were necessary to include the Funding Agency and GM schools within the new legal framework. Section 199 makes truanting an offence and Section 201 makes it the responsibility of the LEA to ensure compliance with the law. This rationalisation was hardly controversial although AMMA and NUT expressed concern about the protracted nature of attendance orders in their comment on the White Paper.

A further aspect of attendance is reflected in concern expressed by the Department for Education (April 1993) which indicated that exclusions had increased by one third in the previous two years (Rogers 1993). The Act now ensures that a fixed term exclusion is limited to 15 days in a term. Furthermore, when a pupil is permanently excluded, the associated funding goes to the new place of provision. This is intended to act as a disincentive to schools' suspending in order to alleviate a problem they cannot address other than by abdication and prevarication. Excluded pupils will go to pupil referral units, which will provide suitable education and, after a reasonable period for assessment, they will be transferred back to a mainstream school or, where necessary, a special school. This fits with the objectives of full attendance and proper enforcement of the law, whilst conforming with the main thrust of the sections dealing with special needs.

With regard to schools failing to give an accepted standard of education, response to the Act was more vitriolic as standards in school rest in the first instance with governors and heads, the power of whom had been consistently reviewed in legislation of the 1980s. As recently as 1992, the Schools Act had established a new system of inspection and the criteria for inspection had been set out in the 'Framework for the Inspection of Schools' 1992. Nonetheless, Government wished to have further procedures for tackling 'failing schools', which were set out in 'Choice and Diversity' Chapter 11.

Where Inspectors' reports identify schools 'at risk' of failing to provide an acceptable standard of education, LEAs were given additional power to deal with the problem, eg, by the right to appoint additional Governors and withdraw delegation. Should this action fail in the view of the Secretary of State, he is now empowered to bring in an Education Association to put the school under new and, significantly, nominated management until performance is deemed satisfactory. Alternatively, the Education Association can propose closure. This will apply to as many schools in an area as are thought to be failing. Clearly, objections were raised to yet another quango further diminishing LEA powers and the automatic transfer to the GM sector when the school is deemed to be performing satisfactorily. The AMA and ACC drew attention to local authority experience in providing support in such circumstances. The Society of Education Officers doubted the ability to turn such a school round when governors, heads and LEA had failed.

The London Boroughs' Association, not surprisingly, drew attention to yet another non-elected nominated body. Standards were to be used as a vehicle to increase centralisation and reflect government doubt and disdain for LEA control mechanisms. Few commentators however highlighted the increasing likelihood of schools failing, given social differences in catchment areas. This is reinforced by open enrolment, accompanied by league tables and increased choice to be exercised by parents whose primary concern is their children irrespective of any consequences to the school. The failure to attract a cross-section of children will quite likely have a comparable effect on staff recruitment, all of which is likely to accelerate the downward spiral of decline which the newly created system has made endemic.

The Act ends on the same note as it begins, with miscellaneous sections involving more unfinished business addressing current issues in an ad hoc manner consistent with a Bill that involved so little consultation and which required consideration of 1,000 amendments in the Lords and a further 500 in the Commons - in all 160 hours of Parliamentary time. Apart from the amendments and codification, it opened up wholly new agendas for division, hardly an adequate foundation for education to take us into the next millennium. To deal with the issue of surplus provision, the Act enables the Secretary of State to direct an LEA, FAS or governors to publish proposals to alter or close schools. If not satisfied, the Secretary of State may publish his own.

The Government estimate that there are 1.5 million surplus places. The Audit Commission estimates the surplus to have cost £140 million in 1990. This addition to the Secretary of State's powers was welcomed by the CBI, but criticised by most of the teacher unions, Catholic Education Council and the Association of Heads of GM schools. Such reactions one might regard as predictable, given the obvious vested interests, but the teachers interestingly point to the surplus as being a pre-requisite for choice which for the most part they deplore. There is no doubt that the scale of the surplus is hugely wasteful but the Government's demonstrable willingness to grant GM status to schools proposed for closure is hardly an even-handed way of dealing with the problem. Notwithstanding the preclusion of schools intended for closure applying for GM status, other measures allow GM schools to change character or size whenever a Local Authority proposes a reorganisation.

The miscellaneous Sections 238 and 239 grant the status of incorporation to school governing bodies. This gives even more power and responsibility to governors, largely at the LEA's expense. It adds to the burdens of time, understanding and responsibility, which asks even more of unpaid volunteers. The net result is likely to be more resignations, unwillingness to volunteer or increasing default and deference to the professional management of the school, which has a long tradition in our system. Sections 241-3 combine the roles of the National Curriculum Council and the Schools Examination and Assessment Council with the creation of the Schools Curriculum and Assessment Authority. In addition it provides a more flexible basis for operating National Curriculum and Assessment procedures. This is undoubtedly an outcome of the protracted conflict reflected in a series of reports from Sir Ron Dearing over an eighteen month period.

The Secretary of State, deeply concerned about sex and religious education, has pronounced as follows: All secondary schools must provide sex education. Governing bodies must make their policies on the subject available to parents and various facets of this topic are excluded from the National Curriculum for Science but must be covered elsewhere. Meanwhile, parents are allowed to withdraw children from such lessons unless they are part of the National Curriculum.

With regard to Religious Education the Act requires that LEAs must, amongst other things, reconvene their agreed Syllabus Conference and reconstitute the Standing Advisory Council on RE to reflect broadly the strength of different denominations and religions. This seems in line with social and cultural, including religious, changes in society. However, LEAs must reflect the fact that the RE tradition in Britain is in the main Christian whilst taking account of the practices of other principal religions. The Secretary of State is clearly anxious about the looseness and variability that previous legislation allowed with regard to sex and religious education. This attempt to clarify the situation may be in accord with his strong views but changing social values suggest that the two issues will be re-addressed soon and perhaps frequently, to keep pace with varying perceptions and changing degrees of religious conviction.

The paradoxes of the Government's ideological inclination are epitomised in the requirement to determine the suitability of people to teach in CTCs and independent schools including what had been considered child care homes. Control from the centre in this regard is for the first time required in the safe haven of the private sector but the Government has given itself the discretion to apply other criteria than those which apply in the public sector. Nonetheless, this is a surprising innovation for a Government associated with privatisation and deregulation. Clearly there is no wish to change the private sector in any significant way and this is evident in the continuing legality of corporal punishment in private schools. Not wishing to exercise total control, the Government has outlawed corporal punishment in the private sector only if it can be deemed 'inhuman and degrading', which brings Britain reluctantly in line with the European Convention of Human Rights.

Is there a framework to carry us into the 21st century?

The mood of the final part of the Act is in line with most of its other sections, being an attempt to rationalise ideological themes. But it gives the impression of tidying, tinkering and tampering in order to ensure that the foundations of the Education Reform Act are buttressed, reinforced and refined so that together they restructure the educational system for the perceivable future. This Act can hardly be described by itself as a watershed although it clarifies some aspects of the Education Reform Act 1988, but if we regard the two as an attempt at fundamental restructuring we may assume that they will lead us to the end of the Century. On the other hand, there are so many outstanding issues relating to the character of the new system, its values, balance and relationships that it seems fair to suggest that this is a structure likely to entrench an ideological divide rather than form the basis for a lasting settlement: an inevitable consequence of this interpretation of choice and diversity.

References

Assistant Masters and Mistresses Association, *Commenting on the White Paper*.

Association of County Councils (1992), *Response to the White Paper*.

Association of Metropolitan Authorities (1992), *Choice and Diversity: Response*.

Audit Commission (1992), *Rationalising Primary School Provision*.

Audit Commission and HMI (1992), *Getting in on the Act: provision for pupils with special educational needs - the national picture*. HMSO

Baroness Blatch, Standing Committee, 20 April 1993, vol 544, No 127,

Official Report, Hansard.

Department for Education (1992), *Special Educational Needs: access to the system.*

Department for Education (1992), *Choice and Diversity: a new framework for schools.* Cm 2021, HMSO.

Department for Education, Press Notice (1992), *Action to Reduce Surplus Places*, 27 August.

Jarvis, F. (1993), *Going, Going, Gone.* Education.

London Borough Associations (1992), *Response to the White Paper.*

National Association of Governors and Managers (1992), *Response to the White Paper.*

National Union of Teachers (1992), *Response to the White Paper.*

National Union of Teachers (1992), *Government White Paper: a Commentary.*

Rogers, R. (1993), *A Guide to the Education Act, 1993.* Advisory Centre for Education.

Society of Education Officers (1992), *Response to the White Paper.*

Warnock Report, Special Education Needs (1978), *Report of the Committee of Enquiry into the Education of Handicapped Children and Young People.* Cmnd 7212, HMSO.

10 The necessity of NCVQ

Lewis Owen

Abstract

This paper maintains that, though there are many problems with the competence model of the curriculum and with the NVQ/GNVQ system of education and training, this approach to the long-standing crisis in the education and training systems of this country is essential, if we are to remain as an advanced industrial society in an era of global capitalist markets. Britain has been involved in long-term industrial decline throughout this century; a critical feature of that decline is the failure to optimise the development of our human resources. The paper argues that this problem is very difficult to remedy because a caste-like professional elite, which began to develop in the nineteenth century but which has increased its influence markedly during the post-war era, continues to prevent the radical changes necessary to remedy the situation. This 'policy community' sincerely believes that it is acting in the best interests of the people of this country, in spite of clear evidence to the contrary. What the new system does is to bypass the old forms of power and make important changes of practice possible.

Introduction

The case for setting up a system such as that presided over by the NCVQ is incontrovertible. Without such a system we would rapidly become a relatively poor and degraded country.

Due mainly to the loss of manufacturing, we face a crisis which is potentially catastrophic. The World Competitiveness Report (cited in The Guardian - Comment, 22/6/93) shows that, in terms of widely accepted criteria, Britain is drifting down the league of the world's twenty-two industrial nations to the bottom. In 1992-93 alone, Britain slipped from

13th to 19th place in terms of the category of 'domestic economic strength', putting us below Spain, Portugal and Finland. In the category of 'science and technology' we dropped from 12th to 13th place; we are 9th in 'finance and internationalisation of the economy', but 22nd in 'industrial production' and 21st in 'funding research and development'. Overall we are judged to have slipped in the last year from 13th to 16th place. While I accept in general the validity of the present government's claims in a recent report (HMSO 1994, pp10-12 and pp30-50) that Britain has made significant relevant changes in its educational and industrial structure, that report does not in any way contradict the argument in the World Competitiveness Report that over the eleven years to 1993 British manufacturing output had risen by only 15% compared to 25% in Germany and 55% in Japan. Alarmingly, we have fewer qualified engineers than any other industrialised nation. The report says that we are de-industrialising because we are weak in skills development, education, motivation and attitudes; our value system has become downgraded, and 'British people have the least energy and enthusiasm in the whole of the industrialised world'. In terms of added value, the report says that Britain is ahead of only Greece, Ireland and Portugal, and that its senior management is considered to be incompetent. Such criticism, if valid, points to the presence of serious structural/systemic problems rather than to the mere lack of competence by individuals.

A key measure of the effectiveness of the 'competence' strategy is not only whether it is theoretically sound, though that is an extremely important question, but also whether it is effective in helping to resolve these structural problems. Nor are these particularly recent problems. In a New Society article (2/1/87), Peter A. Hall makes the point that there has been a continuous if gradual rundown in Britain's industrial competitiveness for about 140 years, since Britain entered what Hobsbawm (1969, p137) called the 'second phase' of industrialisation. This was the phase of heavy capital investment, when our industrial competitors, learning from our experiences, improved on our production systems, with the help of our experts, and inaugurated a process of continuous improvement that we have only ever accepted patchily, particularly when forced by circumstances such as the two world wars. John Eatwell (1982) argues that those institutions and ideologies set up during the era of our industrial pre-eminence have been far too slow to change. In my view this has allowed influential class factions to impose and maintain, not necessarily deliberately, a stranglehold over institutions important to British development, such as those concerned with education and training and finance.

I am not able to consider the financial issues here, of course, but they should always be kept somewhere in mind. All that I am seeking to do is to explore some facets of education and training, an area equally as important as finance. An essential part of the necessary conditions for economic success as a modern technological country is an education and training system capable of providing a workforce whose skills can be rapidly updated to any level required by new technology. The sufficient conditions require that this workforce is part of a highly civilised community whose developed tastes and interests raise the level of cultural life socially, psychologically and physically, and also that it organises cultural production and consumption in ways that make optimal use of the technical advances of the economy. An education and training system that does not meet these necessary and sufficient conditions will inevitably fail to motivate the population as a whole and also create wasted resources and threaten our economic survival.

> Today our companies face the most competitive environment they have ever seen. Change is relentless and swift. The global financial market never sleeps. Technology has shrunk the world. Free trade has opened new markets but it has also created new competitors. We cannot ignore these changes. To do so means certain decline. (HMSO 1994, p3)

These words appear above the name of John Major, but this particular question is not a question of party politics; it is indicative of a situation that all political parties recognise. Whether a competence-based 'accountable' education and training system can significantly help us to solve these problems is not an easy question to answer. It is a question that has to be addressed in terms of the deep structure of the problems that face us rather than the presenting problems. In order to understand what that deep structure might be, it is useful to consider the concept of a 'historical' or 'ideological bloc' (Gramsci 1971, pp60-61), as a way of understanding the log-jam of social, political and ideological factors that appear to have trapped us in institutional rigidities for well over a hundred years. Gramsci makes the point that

> the intellectuals of the historically (and concretely) progressive class, in the given conditions, exercise such a power of attraction that, in the last analysis, they end up by subjugating the intellectuals of other social groups; they thereby create a system of solidarity between all the intellectuals, with bonds of a psychological nature (vanity etc) and often of a caste character (technico-juridical, corporate etc).

There can be little doubt that part of the extraordinary success of the British industrial revolution lay in its intellectual elite, largely members of a composite group of 'modern' technically creative people and a scientific elite with its origins in the late Renaissance and the Enlightenment. They supported the interests of the British bourgeoisie of the 18th and 19th centuries, and they undoubtedly came to dominate the values of the whole of the education and training system. This intellectual elite was, and its descendants still are, in their own sphere, astonishingly successful. For example, in the World Competitiveness Report, we are rated 2nd in terms of numbers of Nobel Prize winners the industrialised countries get. It does, however, have the character of a ruling intellectual 'caste', with a right not just to lead the intellectual vanguard but also to determine the details of the organisation and control of the education and training system from top to bottom. Where it does not have control, ie, over the 'lower' end of the training system, then it makes it very difficult for those who come through that part of the system to access the higher levels. I believe that this elite, whose base is in the universities and professional bodies, is still a highly innovative and progressive force, providing it is situated in a more appropriate, democratic relationship with the rest of society within today's dramatically changed economic and political conditions. The main problem is how this critical balance between leadership and democratic accountability can be achieved and maintained.

Much of the apparently piecemeal change that Britain has undergone in Vocational Education and Training (VET) over the last twenty years was triggered by the catalytic shocks generated by OPEC with its sudden quadrupling of the price of oil in 1973, but the attempt to reform the education and training institutions goes back to at least the Fisher Act (1918), because successive government commissions have recognised the existence of a serious structural problem and vainly tried to remedy it. The Fisher proposals were very far-sighted in that they argued that every child should have a uniform education in grammar schools till the age of 15, designed to prepare the population for industrial systems that were bound to depend more and more on scientific and technological developments. This is of course very like the current Japanese system of Junior Secondary schools.

The proposals were defeated by a combination of factory owners and the labour movement for both of whom the solution to our industrial problems lay in having cheap labour, enabling us to survive in an increasingly competitive world without massive investment costs by industrialists and workers. Our technological success was assumed to be guaranteed, given the technological and scientific creativity of the universities, the rest being left to the inventiveness and energy of our entrepreneurs.

I don't want to imply, by talking of a 'caste-like' educational elite, that the answer to our problems is to look for some specific group of people on which to lay blame or for a single answer to why we have allowed the situation to develop as far as this. This would be a mistake, since, once in a downward spiral, everything tends to conspire unwittingly to the same downward trend. What is important about the 'historical/ideological bloc' as characterised here is its pivotal position in the economy and social structure.

In Gramsci's terms, once established, the ideological bloc absorbs all sorts of related groupings, value systems, and practices, and this becomes a sort of Gordian knot where blame is quite irrelevant, and where what matters is simply cutting the knot apart. This is why the ideological attack on teachers as a group for the manifest crisis in our education system is misdirected; teachers are socialised into a pre-existing system of educational practices. As Giddens (Cohen 1989, p51) observes, 'many social practices in day to day life are performed without being directly motivated .... practices which do not involve an obvious motive occur when agents draw up tacitly understood forms of knowledge.' The answer is simply to alter the terms of reference so that these everyday pedagogic practices become problematised. The way to deal structurally with the schools' part in the maintenance of a highly dysfunctional system is what the state has already done, with the institution of the National Curriculum, SATs, NVQs and so on, coupled with a rigorous critique, on which the state is curiously silent, of the biologistic, psychologistic, deterministic ideology that writes off half the population academically as being 'unintelligent'.

The NVQ/GNVQ system as the key element in changing education's terms of reference seems to have begun to challenge some of the power structures clustered around the ideological bloc. Because it is concerned with assessment rather than with the actual processes of education and training then it can, for example, bypass the power of the colleges and the schools to decide what trainees will need and what they will get, and instead make the schools and colleges answerable to the needs of industry as these change. The lead body system seems to ensure that the most progressive firms from each industry, with their eyes on the performance of global companies, make the running. Of course this is problematic; what if industrial management carries on with its traditional short termism, for example? The way to deal with those sorts of problems, however, is to work forward through them, not to turn back to a system that we know doesn't work for the vast majority of our needs.

Before the inauguration of the new system, it was clear that there had not been enough investment in manufacturing and in research and development (for example, £70 billion in physical capital investment and £33 billion on training - Institute of Policy Studies 1989, p28). Nor has this problem gone away.

The main reason, manufacturers have said, ever since surveys were taken after the war, why they do not invest in modernisation, is the lack of people educated and trained well enough to justify the investment. According to the Institute of Policy Studies (1989, pp8-16), a traditional, coping, non-strategic view of training seemed to have become the predominant attitude within British industry. In 1986/87 there was a total of 2.5 million 16-18 year olds; of these 30% were in full-time education, 16% on the Youth Training Scheme, 7% on part-time day release and 10% attending evening classes. The contribution to this training by employers was very small. The comparison with Germany, the USA and Japan is an unfavourable one, where 80% of the age group are in full-time education and training. Most training by British employers tends to be brief and based on short-term needs rather than long-term objectives. The contribution of industry to training (£18.1 billion pa) is small compared with the benefits it gains and very small compared with the benefits it might gain. Any Vocational Education and Training (VET) system in this country has to deal with the Realpolitik of this, and it has to persuade and/or compel employers to invest far more in VET than they do at present. Those who don't do this will be forced to organise work at lower skill levels and with lower added value production. This will put them into competition with countries such as China and India, whose wage levels are extremely low compared with ours. The consequences for the living standards of workers with low skill levels can be readily envisaged.

We have to judge the NVQ system by these measures - its ability to persuade employers to invest significantly large amounts of resources in VET, and whether it is the sort of flexible system that will enable us to educate and train people quickly and economically enough to the level of the existing requirements of the workforce, no matter what pattern that takes and no matter how rapidly it changes. So we require a VET system that can simultaneously develop human resources at many different levels, yet be flexible enough to upgrade people very quickly to new levels, to enable them to transfer across functional boundaries, acquire new abilities and so on.

The NVQ system certainly appears to make this possible, with its concept of five different levels at each of which equivalences can be established between academic and vocational achievement, whether acquired through study or through practice, and where the recognition of prior experience and learning (hence progression) is built in. As a structure for replacing the anarchy of numerous validation bodies whose qualifications were rarely allowed to be transferred one to another; of a system that sharply divided the vocational and academic, generally giving a far higher prestige to the academic; that failed usually to recognise the achievements of people at work, the NVQ system seems to me both infinitely more rational and humane and far more effective as a vehicle for strategic planning of human resources at a time of economic crisis.

An example will perhaps indicate the way in which the new VET systems work. In an interview (10 July, 1993) with Andrew Pincott, of the International Section of BTEC, Mohammad Amin bin Hamat, then a student seconded by the Malaysian Ministry of Education to the Huddersfield School of Education full-time MEd course, was told of the extraordinary speed of response now possible in BTEC. Mr Pincott gave the example of a group of employers who requested BTEC to set up a Mechatronics training course. Because of the increasing flexibility of the BTEC organisation (it will soon be a private company accountable only to NCVQ), staff were able to work with the employers, students and FE tutors to design and operationalise the course within five months. Even in Germany such courses would require a lead time of two years.

Such flexibility is critical at all levels, particularly in the design of training. The Institute of Policy Studies (1989, pp15-16) claimed that only two thirds of the workforce had any qualifications, while only 14% were considered to be of 'A' level standard, comparing badly with the workforces of the other OECD countries. Under the impact of the new system, that is beginning to change, though perhaps not rapidly enough. The question is whether the competence model can help to cut the Gordian knot of the practices of the historical/ideological bloc that have held us back for over a century, fast enough to enable us to compete in the global economy before it is too late, by rapidly upgrading our education and training system.

What has been taking place in British education over the last few years does have revolutionary implications. From being one of the most elitist systems in the advanced world, the structure that has been rapidly and painfully put into place offers us the opportunity to create a skilled and educated population from top to bottom, not confining it to the top 20% of the population, what Anthony Heath calls the 'salariat'.

> The arguments for and against the Conservative proposals obscure, however, what research has shown: that class inequalities in British education have been remarkably stable throughout the century and that the educational reforms that have so far been attempted - the 1944 Act and free secondary education for all, comprehensive education and the raising of the school leaving age - have made little impact on these inequalities. (Heath 1987, pp13-15)

For the traditional university entrants and those at technician level we have probably had an educational provision that is as good as anywhere in the world, at least since World War Two. But it has become increasingly evident that for everybody else, educational achievements have been very small, something that until very recently (we now have the 'highest graduate output in Europe' HMSO 1994, p39) has been more and more embarrassing each year as other countries make steady improvements in their systems, showing that the problems are not in the intellectual capacities of the learners but in the characteristics and outcomes of those systems.

There is abundant statistical as well as qualitative evidence of the systemic effects of the way we run education. While the mobility studies conducted during the 1970s and 1980s showed that the gaps between the various layers of the system (Heath's 'salariat', 'intermediate class' and 'manual working class') had not altered over the century, this is not the case with countries like America, Germany and especially Japan, where, whatever the faults of their systems, they have for a long time managed to keep the channels of social mobility open, with a consequently much higher general level of education for the mass of the population, and also a much higher output of trained personnel.

Explanations for this are various, but a careful look at any major educational report, from Hadow in 1926 until the significant changes in the Education Reform Act (1988), shows that the ideological consensus of the educators contributing to those reports was almost invariably that the population is composed of three genetically distinguishable groups, so that only about a third of the population was assumed to be able to benefit from the sort of resources that ought to be devoted to people capable of thinking for themselves. The rest, therefore, it was claimed, should be educated to the level of their 'full potential', (as if we had the faintest idea of what that might be) which was bound to be low (see for example Norwood 1943, Newsom 1963). The Japanese, well aware that their only real resource was their people, abandoned our type of approach in the fifties and developed a remarkably egalitarian system until children reach the age of 15, at which point the whole age group has attained a high level of general education, giving them the basis for further lifelong education and training (Sako and Dore 1988, pp72-81). While the Japanese do not stream these pupils, the Germans do, yet they have an ideology that does not put ceilings on people's capacity to learn, and their tri-partite secondary system is used to optimise the different ways that children tend to learn but with the idea that progression up the education ladder is for all.

Ideology seems to be critical as a major factor in the way that systems reproduce themselves. I am taking the meaning of ideology to be that of a general unquestioning view of society, which takes basic propositions for granted, not seeking to establish their validity in any properly scientific way and which therefore suppresses underlying social contradictions, making them invisible. This is the kind of effect that the unexamined belief in people's having fixed quantities of intelligence which can be easily measured has. This ideology, which dominates most of our education reports over a sixty-year period, and whose roots lie in particular kinds of social control, is still evident throughout our education system. It is common among teachers and lecturers to hear the view, based on little more than impressions shared with other teachers, that certain groups or individuals are unintelligent or ineducable. There is a long history of research going back to the early 1960s (eg, Lacey 1970, pp186-193) of the way that streaming and labelling in school systems generate organisational structures and cultures that transmit relative educational failure to some groups. For that not to be recognised as a very serious issue by all teachers, particularly at a point where we are desperately struggling to create a population educated and trainable enough to compete with the Koreans and Taiwanese let alone the Japanese and Germans, seems to me to point up the idea of suppressing contradictions very clearly.

The obviously dysfunctional persistence of that ideology has its roots at least partly in the remarkable degree of autonomy education has had in relation to the rest of society. That educational policy and practice should have remained so out of contact with the requirements of society over such a long and critical period does require explanation. The idea of the presence of an educational 'policy community' at work inside an 'issue network' (Laffin 1986, pp7-8) is a useful way of thinking about the reasons for this. Whatever one might think in general about the New Right's dubious theoretical position, it has pointed clearly to the existence of professional interest clusters of social agents who are able to manipulate public policy in the light of their own ideologies and interests. Jordan (1981, p8) sees the policy community as that 'comparatively small group of participants that a civil servant might define as being of relevance to any particular policy'. Such participants have to be 'sound', trustworthy, expert in some way, and senior: a clear recipe for Conservative policy formulation. A succession of surprisingly elitist and reformist rather than radical governments from both major parties since the war has allowed, in response to an obviously critical shortfall of educated and trained human resources, the policy community to produce what were claimed to be 'revolutionary' reforms - such as ROSLA and comprehensivisation of the school system. All that happened was that the practices of the policy community were never fundamentally altered, and because the old elitist ideology was never seriously challenged at the official level, then it persisted into the culture and practices of the new system, and the old bipartite structure, with its tradition of labelling and streaming, re-appeared in the comprehensive schools and polytechnics.

Laffin (1986, p7) sees 'issue networks' as loose collections of individuals and groups with a shared interest in the area concerned, but with no value consensus. In education there has been for decades a vociferous, diverse and articulate issue network, but like all such networks it has not had a value consensus, and there have been a lot of deep conflicts such as that between the writers of the Black Papers (1969) and Education for Democracy (1970), whose contradictory accounts of the education system arose from the distinct values and social locations of the two groups involved. In Laffin's words -

> Consensus and stability are not prime characteristics of networks; they are much more likely to be affected by change than communities. For they encompass competing groups and, in particular, groups that often advocate change of a more radical type than would typically find acceptance in policy communities.

Gramsci (p11) makes the point that

> every 'essential' social class emerging into history from the preceding economic structure, and as an expression of one of the developments of this structure has found, at least in all history up to now, intellectual categories which were pre-existing and which, moreover, appeared as representatives of an historical continuity uninterrupted by the most complicated and radical changes in social and political forms.

Gramsci's formulation of this somehow epitomises the way in which outdated and dysfunctional aspects of the educational system survive even sustained criticism and contrary research findings. Davies (1971, p116) says of the analysis of a particular culture - 'This is bound to involve an analysis of the interrelationships between the organisations themselves, the characteristics of the economy and the political power structure, and communications systems ...' Davies' analysis sees the question of power as existing at two relevant levels - the national, policy community level (the DES, Treasury, LEAs, UGC and so on) and the institutional level, where schools and colleges implement their own distilled version of national policy. At this level it is clearly teachers, some more than others, who have the power, as they do in the examination boards, curriculum development committees and so on.

> The process of elite accommodation reached its apogee during the post-war period when, so it was believed, many policy decisions in education were taken over lunch at the National Liberal Club by a troika consisting of Sir William Alexander, Secretary of the Association of Education Committees,

Sir Ronald Gould, the then General Secretary of the National Union of Teachers, and the Permanent Secretary of the Department of Education. If these three agreed on some item of education policy, it would more often than not be implemented. The centre's privileged access to law-making and control of financial resources would finally ensure the reluctant compliance of hostile local authorities... (Bogdanor 1979)

In order to explain the persistence of a dysfunctional ideology and practice in face of a situation of relative crisis, it is important to understand how professional groups such as teachers might well successfully resist radical change no matter how essential it is; for example, the remarkable resistance of teachers to the imposition of a national curriculum and SATs. Johnson (1972, p51) says

Professionalism arises where the tensions inherent in the producer-consumer relationship are controlled by means of an institutional framework based upon occupational authority.

Laffin (1986, pp22-23) makes the point that modern professions are mainly organisational professions, and the problems of social control exercised by professions are exacerbated by their intimate involvement in the complexity of such organisations as local government. For the many businessmen and leaders of pressure groups taking up the challenge to the power of the teaching profession over the 'secret garden' of the curriculum (Parkes 1986, p161), they were met with assurances of the profession's trustworthiness and integrity and willingness to engage in dialogue with industry but with little general substantive change taking place. This situation of organisational complexity backed up by moral authority allows members of a professionalising body such as teachers to avoid questions of accountability and competence even in the face of sharp criticism supported strongly by statistical and logistical evidence. Jamous and Pelouille (1970, p29) describe a profession as an occupation whose 'indetermination/technicality ratio, intrinsic to systems of production, is generally high'; that is, the balance between that part of their expertise that is accessible and accountable to their customers and that part that consists of professional mystique. In 1976 the 'secret garden of the curriculum' was where teachers' professional mystique was hidden, and by and large our decisions about the transmission of knowledge and about the abilities of those to whom it is transmitted have been until lately sacrosanct.

The issue of 'competence and accountability' is centrally an issue about who manages knowledge as a relatively scarce resource - those with professional hegemony or the state. The answer depends on whether you think that the state or the body of professionals is more likely to act effectively on behalf of the vast majority of people. There have been periods in recent history when I have strongly felt that the state was incompetent in this field and that significant groups of professionals did see the way ahead more effectively (see Owen and Stoneman in Rubinstein and Stoneman 1970, pp67-81). I do still strongly believe that the representatives of the state should engage much more seriously in dialogue with teachers, but the nature of the human resource/economic crisis is now so serious that only measures as radical as the NVQ system, backed by state power and involving teachers as one interest group among others, seems to me feasible. There really is nothing else on offer worth considering.

What has happened is that the state has formally activated more and more of the 'issue network' for education, by involving industry through the NCVQ and the TECs, parents and the business community via the governors etc, while at the same time narrowing the policy community by taking away the power of the LEAs and the teaching unions and breaking down the conservative elements in the system. It seems reasonably clear that these are the policies of a new historical/ideological bloc.

A new social class and associated class fractions may well have begun to emerge in the economic crises precipitated by the 'oil shocks' of the 1970s and 1980s. Sklair (1993) sees this as a transnational capitalist class, responsive to or associated with the activities of the transnational companies, operating readily across international boundaries, and with an economistic and consumerist ideology. No matter how socialist we might be as individuals, global capitalism is now unchallenged and countries such as Britain have to respond or sink further and further down the league table of rich nations. The ideologies and transnational practices of this new class may offend us deeply, imbued as we are with the elite values of a disappearing constellation of power as well as with ideals based on social equity and community, but we have to evaluate them as objectively as possible, and we have to deal with them constructively, asking which of their practices will enable us to build societies fit for the 21st century. I have argued that in terms of our immediate economic needs the concepts of competence and accountability are essential as ways of instating an educational practice that can cope with the human resource requirements of the near future. To do that a great deal of modification and quite radical changes may be necessary, but the structure is in place that can sweep aside old practices holding us back within an old social order. Of course, we need to be careful that we are not at the same time swept into a new global division of labour where it is acceptable to exploit a national and international underclass instead of a merely national underclass. But that is another struggle.

Reform of the education and training system has then to achieve a number of objectives: it has to be of a kind whose practices break up the old elitist ideology, making it impossible to carry on believing that it is in our best interests as a people to recreate dysfunctional divisions between social classes; concomitantly it has to be of such a kind that it frees up the creative intelligence of people so that they become adaptable and constructive in their approach to both their social roles and the development of their personhood. In order to do these things the resourcing of education and training has to be shared by everyone, since ultimately everyone benefits; this necessarily involves employers as well as the state; it also involves families and individuals whose commitment to learning has previously been made suspect by their ability to slide through the system, playing its games as effectively as possible, rather than seeing learning as an essential social investment for themselves, their families and the community. In order to begin to achieve these things, power needs to be redistributed away from the policy community of state, professionals and local state, to a much more shared power, shared with parents, employers and relevant interest groups within the issue network, but centrally directed because of the challenges presented by the globalisation of the world economic system which can only really be tackled from a national and European perspective.

The NVQ system does at least part of that. At the national level it is led by a combination of government and the large firms, anxious to have a training system that can enable them to respond very rapidly and sensitively to the global challenge. The large firms can therefore see the value of this kind of education and training and so they invest in it, time and expertise as well as money. At the local level the TECs involve and lead smaller employers who in this way are drawn into the resourcing of training and begin to see its point. Whether this always works properly, or whether it works rarely in practice, it can always be improved; the structure is in place for that to happen. The dangers are of course real: the possibility of a quasi-totalitarian division of labour on a continental scale, within a highly exploitative world division of labour. The best way to fight that possibility is to ensure that educational resources are used efficiently to raise the cultural and social levels of the whole population, not a limited elite.

The elitism in our system has been fostered by the sharp division between those who study vocationally or simply work, and those who study academically. This division has spawned numerous examination bodies, and many divisions between courses and institutions, with few routes for career progression. Such a system has been immensely wasteful and very damaging to those who, for whatever reason, have been made to feel intellectually inferior to others. The NVQ system is a serious attempt to break those divisions down. It is argued by many progressive teachers that the old divisions have been recreated, since the old elitist ideology has not gone away and all we have done is to reproduce it in the various levels of the NVQ system. There is some evidence that this may be happening; if so, I feel that it is not merely an indication of the inherent difficulties in the new system, but also of an ideologically constructed rearguard practice by people who are unwilling to make what are essential changes. Those divisions may well survive no matter how open the explicit structure of the system becomes. It very much depends on the nature of the specific ideological and political struggles to reconstruct educational practice that take place at the relevant sites. That is in our own hands and requires us as teachers to bring the best kind of analytical and creative practice to the situations we are in.

The new system goes well beyond structural change. Intrinsic to the NVQ system is the concept of progression and the assessment of prior experience and learning. These two things mean that we have to begin to examine far more deeply what we mean by learning, at its deep structure as well as at its surface structure levels (using this metaphor somewhat differently from the way I used it earlier in this argument) than we have done before. This is no longer therefore a question of whether a group of teachers or examiners arrives at an agreed mark for an examination answer on the basis of their collective experience, but a practice that forces us to examine epistemologically and sociologically the nature of our subjects. Interestingly, today one finds as a teacher educator, for the first time in my own experience, the majority of teachers on the courses that I teach treating these abstract questions as familiar, everyday issues. The very basis of the outcomes model ensures that the question of deep structure is addressed. In order for learning to be made accountable, serious questions have to be asked about how it takes place in ways that will enable it to be the basis for enhanced practice or for transferred practice. In principle this takes theoretical practitioners into quite new areas of activity. I have recently been listening to a tape recording of a team of tutors of GNVQ Manufacturing at Leeds College of Technology talking with one of our MEd students about the way that their section members are having to rethink methods of learning and teaching because of the requirements of the GNVQ curriculum. It is an exciting, creative and deeply thoughtful discussion about the nature of technology, of learning and of pedagogical practice. It is the sort of discussion that all educational professionals would like to be associated with. It is indicative of what the new system is generating in the area of pedagogical practice. It is clear evidence that the outcomes model is not the same sort of model as the objectives model of the curriculum which by-passed knowledge and focussed on behaviour. The outcomes model in the end requires pre-eminently that we address the issue of the nature of knowledge and its transmission and construction.

The other dimension of the concept of competence is that we are pushed towards the notion of an all or nothing threshold of practice beyond which people may become more and more expert and refined but before which they are not considered capable and must therefore undergo further learning. In GNVQ, for example, the pass mark is 70% of criterion mastery (it was formerly higher than this). This is of course highly problematic at the theoretical level, but as a practical device for compelling us to address questions of the nature of knowledge it is excellent. What is more it enables us to set goals for learners, goals that then become sources of motivation. It also entails, in a course with a concept of progression, the breaking down of the knowledge area into those things that come together to compose the particular knowledge form, to assess them as sub-elements in the knowledge and to re-teach them where competence is not achieved. This clearly takes us back to the Mastery Learning ideas of Block (1972, p3).

This model of effective systems of learning claimed remarkable results.

> Mastery learning (Bloom 1968) offers a powerful new approach to student learning which can provide almost all students with the successful and rewarding learning experiences now allowed to only a few. It proposes that all or almost all students can master what they are taught. Further it suggests procedures whereby each student's instruction and learning can be so managed, within the context of ordinary, group-based classroom instruction, as to promote his fullest development. Mastery learning enables 75 to 90 per cent of the students to achieve to the same high level as the top 25 per cent learning under typical group-based instructional methods. It also makes student learning more efficient than conventional approaches. Students learn more material in less time. Finally, mastery learning produces markedly greater student interest in and attitude towards the subject learned than usual classroom methods.

This is one of the ideas that lie at the heart of the NVQ system. It is both a liberating idea, in the sense that it suggests to us that people have far greater capacity to learn than we have heretofore accepted, and also a very practical idea in that it suggests very specific ways in which we can work with people to develop their capacities. It does not have to stay located in the behaviourism that originally generated it, but can be equally applied to far more creative fields simply by altering the practice so that it approximates to the requirements of those fields. This is what GNVQ teachers, under the stimulus of the new curricula, are now doing.

151

Many of the NVQs are unfortunately being conceived and developed far too narrowly. Perhaps this is inevitable given the ideological and practical history of some of the business people setting them up and of some of the teachers, trainers and assessors. Providing that as a society we can bootstrap ourselves appropriately into the 21st century, then that should disappear, because it is unlikely to be adequate for the global, high added value markets we should be aiming for. If we don't master that problem then life could be very nasty for a lot of people. We certainly haven't mastered it at the moment, even in our highly prestigious 'A' level system, which is sometimes little more than an inefficient instruction course in how to pass examinations (35% of candidates end up with nothing after two years). GNVQs credit you with what you've achieved, like NVQs, so it offers all of us hope and the possibility of progress. What is more, by the very act of describing the NVQ levels in such a way that GCSE and GCE 'A' levels, degrees and post-graduate qualifications can be compared with work-based learning, we have demystified the practices of the academy and its disempowering mystique and enabled people to see that they do employ their intelligence in every area of their lives, not just when they sit down and write examination papers and assignments.

References

Block, J.H. (1971), *Mastery Learning. Theory and Practice*. London: Holt, Rinehart and Winston.

Bogdanor, V. (1979), *Power and Participation*. Oxford Review of Education, Vol 5, No 2.

Cohen, I.J. (1989), *Structuration Theory. Anthony Giddens and the Constitution of Social Life*, Contemporary Social Theory. London: Macmillan.

Cox, C.B. and Dyson, A.E. (eds) (1969), *Fight for Education: a Black Paper*. Critical Quarterly Society.

Davies, I. (1971), *The Management of Knowledge: a critique of the use of typologies in education sociology*, in Earl Hopper (ed) 'Readings in the Theory of Educational Systems'. London: Hutchinson.

D.T.I. (1994), *Competitiveness - Helping Business to Win*. London: HMSO.

Eatwell, J. (1982), *Whatever Happened to Britain? The Economics of Decline*. London: Duckworth.

Gramsci, A. (1971), *Selections from the Prison Notebooks of Antonio Gramsci*, edited and translated by Quintin Hoare and Geoffrey Nowell Smith. London: Lawrence and Wishart.

Hall, P.A. (1987), *Decline and Fall*, New Society, 2 January.

Heath, A. (1987), *Class in the Classroom*, New Society, 17 July.

Hobsbawm, E.J. (1969), *Industry and Empire. The Pelican Economic History of Britain*, Vol 3. Harmondsworth: Penguin.

Institute of Policy Studies (1989), *Training in Britain. A Study of Funding Activity and Attitudes. The Main Report*. London: Institute of Policy Studies.

Jamous, H. and Peloille, B. (1970), *Changes in the French University Hospital System*, in Jackson, J.A. (ed), 'Professions and Professionalisation'. Cambridge University Press.

Jordan (1981), *Iron Triangles*, cited in Laffin, 1986.

Lacey, C. (1970), *Hightown Grammar: the school as a social system*. Manchester: Manchester University Press.

Laffin, M. (1986), *Professionalism and Policy: the Role of the Professions in the Central-Local Government Relationship*. London: Tavistock.

Newsom Report (1963), *Half Our Future*. Report of the Central Advisory Council for Education (England), Ministry of Education. London: HMSO.

Norwood Report (1943), *Curriculum and Examinations in Secondary Schools* Report of the Secondary Schools Examinations Council, appointed by the Board of Education, 1941.

Parkes, D.L. (1985), *Competence and Competition*, in McNay, I. and Ozga, J. (eds) Policy-making in Education. Exeter: Wheaton.

Rubinstein, D. and Stoneman, C. (1970), *Education for Democracy*. Penguin Books.

Sako, M. and Dore, R. (1988), *Teaching or Testing: the role of the state in Japan*. Oxford Review of Economic Policy, Vol 4, No 3.

Sklair, L. (1991), *Sociology of the Global System*. London: Harvester Wheatsheaf.

'World Competitiveness Report 1993'. The World Economic Forum.

GOLDMINE

Finding free and low-cost resources for teaching
1995–1996

Compiled by David Brown

"It can be highly recommended because the choice of subjects, the organisation of the entries, and an index make a mass of information very easily accessible. Having used this directory to acquire resources for a couple of ad hoc topic areas, I can confidently state that it works - with ease and practicability. In the saving of teachers' time, let alone in access to materials, it really is a goldmine. I would advise any school to acquire this book. The title of the book is wholly accurate and the outlay is modest compared with the returns." **School Librarian**

David Brown has been teaching in primary, middle and secondary schools for 23 years. It was through David's need to find resources within a limited school budget that he began to uncover a wealth of low-cost, good quality material which was just what he was looking for.

Goldmine places these resources into topic areas, describes them and tells you where you can get them from. Since the first edition in 1985, **Goldmine** has developed into the country's leading directory of free and sponsored teaching resources, providing the wherewithal to obtain over 6000 resources from some 235 suppliers.

Budget-conscious schools will find it saves its purchase price many times over, and parents and teachers are safe in the knowledge that all the items described in here ar personally recommended by a teacher, the compiler himself.

1995   329 pages   1 85742 137 X   £15.00

Price subject to change without notification

arena

50 POPULAR TOPICS

A resources directory for schools

Compiled by David Brown

You are resourcing a topic, and you don't know who publishes what. The school doesn't have all the publishers catalogues you need, and you don't have addresses for those you haven't got.

THE RESOURCES DIRECTORY has been compiled to solve all these problems. The 50 most popular primary and secondary school topics are included with a huge range of books, videos, software, kits, packs, equipment and schemes for all ages between 5 and 13.

Over 2500 items from 50 suppliers are included, together with their addresses, all grouped in topics, cross-referenced in a comprehensive index and with an appendix of schemes in science, technology, geography and history.

David Brown is a schoolteacher with over 20 years teaching experience in primary, middle and secondary schools. He is also author of 'GOLDMINE', published by Arena.

1995   201 pages   1 85742 163 9   £15.00

arena

DEAFNESS, CHILDREN AND THE FAMILY

A GUIDE TO PROFESSIONAL PRACTICE
· ·

Jennifer Densham

This is a research based book intended for professionals in medical, educational, health and social work fields who come into contact with deaf children and their families. Many of the issues raised also have implications for professionals working with parents of children with other forms of disability.

The book illustrates the need for change in some professional practice, and focuses attention on those areas where change may be effected. It covers the impact of deafness, parental reactions to diagnosis, attitudes of professionals and their affect on the communication, education and integration of deaf children, and emotional implications in terms of stigma, self-esteem and socialization.

Jennifer Densham is a freelance lecturer and consultant, and a research supervisor for the University of Hertfordshire, with a small private counselling practice.

1995   224 pages   Hbk   1 85742 221 X   £32.50

Price subject to change without notification

arena